MAYWOOD PUBLIC LIBRARY

3 1312 00203 1496

W9-BLF-778

Maywood Public Library
121 S. 5th Ave.
Maywood, IL 60153

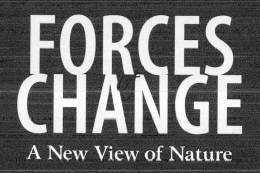

FORCES OF CHANGE

A New View of Nature

Having given up his job as a park ranger, this hunter now tracks traditional game in Africa's Kalahari.

FORCES *of* CHANGE

A New View of Nature

Smithsonian
National Museum of Natural History

IN ASSOCIATION WITH

NATIONAL GEOGRAPHIC

WASHINGTON, D.C.

Observe constantly that all things take place by change,
and accustom thyself to consider that the nature of the Universe
loves nothing so much as to change the things which are
and to make new things like them.

—MARCUS AURELIUS

Contents

Seagoing mammals get up close and personal during a whale-watching encounter off the California coast. Following the animals on their annual north-south transit, tourists eager to engage wildlife in their daily lives venture tantalizingly close and then retreat respectfully.

DANIEL B. BOTKIN

The Nature of Change

In the past decades it has become fashionable to speak of change as natural, and to discuss life from a planetary perspective. New scientific methods and instruments allow us to track changes in the environment—past and present—with ever greater precision; advances in satellite imagery and other technologies allow us to watch global phenomena such as El Niño unfold in real time. We would seem to be well on our way to accepting a new view of nature, one that accommodates its complexity, dynamism, and unpredictability. But changing one's outlook on something as fundamental as nature isn't easy. Older, more comforting beliefs maintain a strong hold on us. Down deep, we still wish for nature's benevolent constancy.

As we move into the new millennium, the headlines present us with stories of impending climate change, ecological crises, and wrenching social changes, making it more important than ever that we come to terms with the idea that change is the rule, not the exception, for life on the Earth. In seeking to conserve and manage our living resources, we must learn how to work within these forces of change. We must learn to replace our idea of static beauty and perfection in biological nature with a new appreciation of the dynamics and processes in ecological systems.

Throughout the history of western civilization, for several thousand years, people have generally believed that there existed a great balance of nature, that nature, left alone, would inevitably achieve a permanent form and a constant structure. "Who cannot wonder at the harmony of things, at this symphony of nature which seems to will the well-being of the world?" wrote the Roman orator and statesman Cicero in the first century B.C. Nature was a still life, perfect and beautiful in its constancy—like the beautiful landscape paintings of the 19th-century Hudson River School, Bierstadt's "Sunset in the Yosemite

Overcoming natural and man-made changes, salmon return to their annual spawning grounds.

Valley" and Church's "Morning in the Tropics." According to this myth, if nature's balance is disturbed, it recovers, attaining once again its original, pristine state. This permanent, fixed condition was believed best for all life, including human beings. There was a divinely ordained place and purpose for every creature, and every creature was in its place—a great, harmonious chain of being.

The balance of nature provided an explanation about how nature worked. But how did nature come about, and if nature was supposed to be perfect, why was it often not that way? A person explains how an unknown thing works based on what he already knows. Before the time of complex machines, what people knew best were living things: their own bodies and the bodies of animals and plants. An ancient answer to how nature worked and why nature was not perfect lay with this explanation, known as the organic myth of nature. In this view, nature is alive, either in fact or metaphorically, operating like a living creature. The imperfections in nature were therefore easily explained: Mother Nature was growing old and less fertile. Mountains were wrinkles on her skin, proof that she was aging.

With the rise of science and modern technology in the 17th and 18th centuries, and the blossoming of science in the 19th and 20th, the organic myth gave way to a new explanation. People now had complex machines as a basis for explanation. The Earth became the great machine created by the omnipotent and omniscient engineer. A new kind of perfection was seen in motion and dynamics, in the beautiful formulation of Newton's laws of motion, in the elegant elliptical paths of the planets through the cosmos.

The new, machine-based view had several important effects on our attitudes toward nature. A machine-nature has a maximum power output and can be run at a steady state. It can be invented and reinvented, engineered and reengineered. Like any 19th-century machine—a waterwheel or clockworks—it could supposedly be explained with a few variables. Machine-nature reinforced belief in the balance of nature. According to both, nature could be maintained in a fixed condition and a variation from this fixed condition was undesirable.

The science of ecology flowered in the 20th century as a child of the machine age, its models, metaphors, and mathematical approaches inherited from engineering and the physical sciences. For natural resources that we wanted to extract and use, the machine myth led to the idea that ecosystems can supply a fixed and predictable level of output, known as the maximum sustainable yield, that we can consistently exploit without fear of depleting the resource. This concept continues to dominate management and conservation practices in applied fields such as fisheries, wildlife, and forest management.

For many years I have followed the way that professional fisheries biologists have recommended managing the world's great fisheries. This management has been a great

Seventeenth-century Jesuit scholar Athansius Kircher visualized the interior of a volcano much as a living organism, with channels of lava serving as its life blood. Such biological metaphors of the Earth, though later supplanted by mechanical metaphors, continue to shape many of our attitudes toward nature.

curiosity, because it has been purposeful, well-meaning, but generally a failure, producing crashes in populations of the fish under management—the decimation of the California sardine industry (immortalized in Steinbeck's *Cannery Row*) in the 1950s, the disastrous crash of the Peruvian anchovy fishery in the 1970s, and the steep decline of Atlantic menhaden, cod, and other commercially important species on the Grand Banks off Newfoundland in the last quarter of the 20th century are spectacular examples. What happened? Operating under the idea of the balance of nature, fisheries managers assumed the environment was constant, and based harvest levels on normal years. But in an

Nature is often hidden; sometimes overcome; seldom extinguished.

—FRANCIS BACON

inherently variable system such as the ocean, what, if anything, is normal? Such a faulty understanding of how nature works inevitably led to overfishing during years of poor upwellings and other natural fluctuations, resulting in eventual failure of the fisheries.

Although professional ecologists and environmental scientists generally agree that some kinds of changes are natural, the balance of nature idea is alive and well, and infiltrates proposals for conservation as well as management. Environmental planners are often urged to seek a static biological landscape, one assumed to have existed thousands of years ago, before the first humans arrived in North America. It is a landscape in which people are interlopers upsetting the balance of nature, destroying what an article in the journal *Conservation Biology* called the "purely natural condition that might serve as an absolute benchmark for planners."

But if nature is always changing, what is natural? If we wish to return a landscape to its natural condition, which of its many conditions should we choose? For much of North America, the condition that persisted for the longest time during the last 30,000 years was a continental ice sheet. Is that what we should choose? Obviously not. Instead, we should realize that for any area there is no single pristine state of nature, as assumed in the balance of nature idea, but rather a set of nature's designs, each of which may have persisted for a thousand years or more and each of which could be considered natural. And within each of these general conditions, short-term changes—fires and storms, for example—are natural as well. We have a choice of what is natural, so long as we allow natural changes to occur.

If the balance of nature idea is so unrealistic, contradicted by so many observations, why does it remain so appealing to many of us? It persists, in part, because of its strong ties with Western religious tradition: a benevolent, perfect, and all-powerful God could only make a perfect world. Seen in this way, to deny nature's perfection is to deny the perfection of God. And aside from the religious connection, the balance of nature idea is also a comforting image of nature. We like to believe that the forests and streams we visited as children will remain the same, with the same fishing holes, abundant wildlife, and familiar trees. A salmon fishermen would like every year to be one of great, unvarying abundance; the old concept of a maximum sustainable yield would suit him just fine if it were possible. People have to make a living, and they want some reliability; a harvest that varies greatly from year to year is not desirable.

The balance of nature idea also persists because of what I call the Pandora's Box Dilemma: If we accept one kind of change as natural, doesn't this open the door to others, bad as well as good? Must we accept them all? But once we understand that nature changes, we can examine the kinds, rates, and amounts of change that are natural. These natural changes can give us a basis for distinguishing the acceptable from the unacceptable. In the history of life on Earth there are kinds of changes that have existed for a long enough time, and have been frequent enough, that species have been able to evolve and adapt to them. If we introduce a change that is natural in kind, rate, and amount, then it is likely to be benign. If we introduce a change that is novel in kind, rate, or amount, then we need to be concerned, because species have not had an opportunity to evolve and adapt to it. Its effects are likely to be undesirable. For example, there is nothing in nature like a plow, and we should be careful in our use of plowing, even though this is, from a human perspective, an ancient technology. Chemicals that never existed before human invention, but which our modern technology releases into the environment, must be treated with great care. But, unfortunately, this goes against still another reason that many of us cling to the balance of nature idea: It provides an easy solution to the problems of management and conservation, one that requires no knowledge. If nature unerringly maintains itself in a state of perfect balance, then the solution to all environmental problems would be to leave nature alone. Nature would know best. It would always return itself to that single state that was best for itself and for us.

It is clear what we must do, but it will be hard to do it. We have to accept the naturalness and inevitability of change. But we must also understand the patterns of natural change. We must understand the natural set of states of being and how rapidly it can shift. This requires regular and sound scientific observations and measurements on all scales of space and time, from the fall of a tree in a forest to global changes over millennia. But to support such research and maintain such records will require an unprecedented degree of commitment and cooperation from all sectors of society.

The transition that we are going through today for biological nature is analogous to the 17th- and 18th-century transition for the cosmos. Then, new observations of the motion of the planets showed that changes were natural, and that they followed explicit, understandable, and beautiful rules. Today we are struggling to accept new conceptions of change in biological nature. The transition is more difficult, because biological nature is made up of complex systems we barely understand and for which we do not yet have a set of formal, mathematical rules comparable to Newton's laws of motion. Indeed, the complexity of ecological systems may never allow such elegance and simplicity. But perhaps as we learn to accept their complexity and their dynamism, we can see in them a new kind of order, a new source of beauty and inspiration. The powerful images and insights in this book can help us through this transition, and open our minds to a new, dynamic view of nature.

Introduction

ALAN CUTLER

New Frontiers,
New Explorations

T hree and a half centuries after Columbus crossed the Atlantic and made his historic landfall in the West Indies, six small wooden ships departed from Hampton Roads, Virginia, on a voyage around the world. Officially called the United States South Seas Exploring Expedition and led by Lt. Charles Wilkes, it was the young republic's first venture overseas with the explicit purpose of scientific discovery. When the ships set sail in August 1838, on board was a youthful band of naturalists, scientists, ethnographers, artists, and cartographers.

During the four-year voyage, the scientific team collected thousands of natural history specimens—birds, mammals, corals, mollusks, plants, minerals, rocks, and fossils, many of them new to science. They painted portraits of Polynesian royalty and amassed cultural objects by the crate. They compiled data on the winds and currents of the Pacific Ocean and produced hundreds of charts and maps. But the single most momentous event came two years into the voyage. Three of the ships were probing the cold, uncharted waters far to the south of Australia, when lookouts spied the blue peaks of mountains looming above the ice on the southern horizon. Others sailing in the far South had made landfalls on islands and desolate points of land, but Wilkes and his companions were the first to surmise that what they had found was a vast, unexplored continent. They proceeded to map more than 1,400 miles of coastline.

The continent was Antarctica, the last of the world's great landmasses to become known to man. After thousands of years of dispersal and migration around the globe, crossing continents, hopping from island to island, our wandering species had at last, almost literally, reached the end of the Earth. Human populations had long before found their way to the remotest Pacific islands. They had carved niches for themselves in the rain forests

Salt crystals from a meteorite reveal water—an essential ingredient of life.

Indeed, what is Nature but change, in all its visible,
and still more its invisible processes?

—WALT WHITMAN

of Amazonia and the severe environments of Tibet, the Sahara, and the high Arctic. And during this time the Antarctic continent had remained unknown and untouched.

Today, when there is more information available about Antarctica than any one person could ever hope to absorb, and when, for a price, one can visit Antarctica, it is difficult to imagine the thoughts and emotions of these 19th-century voyagers as they skirted the fringe of a newfound continent. And given the rigors of handling a sailing ship in the rough polar seas, perhaps few of them stopped to ponder the broader implications of their discovery. Certainly none would have perceived the fragility of the Antarctic environment or been able to foresee how quickly commercial seal and whale hunting would deplete its abundant marine mammal populations, driving some species nearly to extinction before the century's end.

But the start of a new millennium provides an opportunity to consider how new ideas, new discoveries, and the accelerating pace of change fit into the larger patterns of nature and human history. Looking ahead to the new century, preparing for its challenges and uncertainties, is perhaps a little like glimpsing a new continent on the horizon—the vista is expansive and exciting, but more than a little overwhelming, too.

This book was inspired by "Forces of Change," a program of exhibits, public events, and publications designed by the Smithsonian's National Museum of Natural History, intended as a forum where scientists, scholars, writers, and the public could explore a broad range of scientific and social questions, relating to change, both natural and human-induced. The growing public awareness of potential climate shifts, diminishing biodiversity, and other environmental and social issues is enough to make change a timely and provocative theme. But the complexity of the issues that confront us and of the underlying forces of change leads inevitably to more basic questions—questions regarding our relationship with nature and our complicated, often ambivalent, attitudes toward change.

Answers that have emerged so far often come from unexpected places. The frozen, austere continent encountered by the Wilkes Expedition has become the focus of intense scientific research, a unique natural laboratory of global change. In its ice is a record of the world's climate, written in layers of dust, gas bubbles, and chemical variations that extend back tens of thousands of years. Its sediments and rock strata constitute an archive of evolution, extinction, and geological change spanning hundreds of millions of years. Answers to questions about the history (and future) of the world's oceans, the evolution of Australia's strange animals, and the global cataclysm that wiped out the dinosaurs may be found on the Antarctic continent and beneath its surrounding

City in the clouds of the Andes, Machu Picchu is a spectacular example
of a population center that thrived for a time—then fell into utter disuse.
Natural changes or cultural evolution can transfer a metropolis into
a mausoleum within the span of just a few generations.

seas. And despite the continent's isolation, reports of DDT in the flesh of Antarctic
penguins, the waxing and waning of ozone holes, and scenarios of global warming and ice
sheet collapse attest to its continuing intimate link with the affairs of the rest of the
planet—and its surprising vulnerability to human disturbance.

The Earth is a vast, dynamic, complex, and highly interconnected system. For convenience, and by habit, we sort the many different aspects of this system into scientific
categories—geology, chemistry, meteorology, biology, anthropology, and economics. The
Earth's natural systems and subsystems, however, have no respect for such intellectual
boundaries—its processes and elements form an interactive whole. The minerals in a soil,
the acidic rainwater soaking into the ground, the roots of a plant, and a gardener's metal
spade all converge in a flower bed to yield prize-winning zinnias under certain conditions. The soil alone is far too complex a mixture of humus, clay minerals, water, and
dissolved ions for the categories "biological," "geological," or "chemical" to be of much
use. And are the cultivated flowers—combined products of years of selective breeding and
millions of years of natural selection—artificial or natural?

The connections of a suburban garden system extend far beyond the edge of its tilled soil. The sand, silt, and clay of the soil might have been brought to this spot by an ancient river or glacier, with perhaps an admixture of dust carried here by the wind from a desert on another continent. To counteract the soil's acidity the gardener may add particles of limestone, derived from the residue of fossil algae or an ancient reef that was quarried, pulverized, packaged, and then trucked across the country.

At the sunny edge of this garden, there is a shrub with shiny leaves and pink blossoms. The shrub, a rosy periwinkle, is native to the dry forests of Madagascar, island of lemurs and other evolutionary exotica. The gardener's niece, recently diagnosed with leukemia, is being treated with vincristine, a medication derived from an extract of rosy periwinkle plants. And although the higher levels of carbon dioxide put into the air by the burning of fossil fuels haven't helped the garden plants to grow noticeably faster, the spate of unusually severe summer droughts has certainly made it hard to raise a decent vegetable crop the past few seasons. When the gardener reads in her newspaper's science section that unusual weather during recent austral summers has made it tough for penguins on the Antarctic Peninsula to raise their chicks, she may or may not make a connection with the wilted tomatoes in last summer's garden.

The complexity, unpredictability, and inherent dynamism of nature in all its manifestations run counter to the expectations and desires of many people. In 1990 Daniel Botkin published a provocative and influential book, *Discordant Harmonies*, in which he explored our often idealistic perceptions of nature and our misguided desire for constancy and harmonious balance in nature. These misperceptions, arising from religious, cultural, and psychological roots, hamper our ability to understand natural systems. And unless these outmoded beliefs are discarded, Botkin argued, they will continue to thwart our best efforts to deal effectively with today's environmental challenges and those we confront in the new millennium. A gardener trying to control aphids with pesticides and a scientist trying to predict the future stability of the West Antarctic ice sheet with a computer simulation are in comparable predicaments—there are just too many variables and unknowns to know for sure what nature will do next.

Botkin pointed out several aspects of natural systems that are particularly difficult for people to accept and that are often ignored or inadequately considered in scientific investigations and by environmental policies. The first is the prevalence and universality of change. As Dorion Sagan and Eric Schneider observe in this book, change is a fundamental property of life. All living things depend on a constant flow of energy and exchange

Humans may see a wilderness such as Minnesota's Boundary Waters region (above) as a pristine example of nature in balance—but not long ago glaciers scoured this landscape. Similarly, billions of bison hooves (below) and the animals' grazing habits helped shape America's prairies.

You cannot step twice into the same river,
for other waters are continually flowing in.

—HERACLEITUS

of matter to survive. Adaptation and change are the primary business of life. And the physical Earth, as geologists have come to learn in the 20th century, and as William Melson describes, is equally dynamic, though on a far longer timescale. Over the billions of years that our planet has been in existence, huge plates of its crust have shifted and jostled one another, mountain ranges have risen and fallen like breaking waves, and the world's climate has fluctuated between greenhouse and icehouse conditions. In parts of the world most recently covered by continental ice sheets, such as Canada and areas of Northern Europe, ecosystems are still recovering from the glacial conditions and the crust, formerly weighed down by miles of ice, is still rebounding to its former elevation. Every place has a history; for no region or location in the world can it be said that there is a single, pristine, natural state, or a stable, unvarying, normal climate. Climatologists such as Jonathan Overpeck are finding that through the millennia, large areas of the globe have been abruptly jolted by rapid changes in climate—climate surprises—and there is no reason not to expect more of these in the future.

Many of us have difficulty accepting such uncertainty or believing that chance can play such an important role in nature. This attitude has roots in religious doctrine, what Botkin refers to as the divine order of nature, but it is also an outgrowth of the methods and assumptions of classical physics, epitomized by Isaac Newton's deterministic "clock-work" universe, in which the natural world worked in perfect synchrony, like the inner workings of a pendulum clock. Scientists have come a long way since Newton's time—chance and probability are key aspects of Darwin's theory of natural selection, the laws of thermodynamics, quantum theory in physics, and other modern theories—but the influence of Newton and his mechanistic assumptions remains strong. To scientists, engineers, policy makers, and taxpayers, uncertainty and frankly probabilistic answers to questions can appear unscientific and evasive, yet predicting disease and pest outbreaks, earth-quakes, and hurricanes is complicated by uncertainties inherent to the natural forces that make these events happen.

Related to our discomfort with chance and the unpredictability of changes is the assumption that they are somehow unnatural or inevitably destructive. Stephen Jay Gould spent the better part of his career championing the idea that quirky, punctuational change is at least as much the norm in nature as is gradual, linear change: Organisms can evolve and form new species in sudden, unpredictable bursts of change after eons of stability. Likewise, a zspecies can become extinct as the result of a random, catastrophic event, such as an asteroid impact, regardless of the Darwinian fitness it enjoyed during better times. Ecologists are now also recognizing the value of "disturbance"—fires, storms, and floods—in maintaining the health and biodiversity of some ecosystems. Many species can survive only in periodically disturbed habitats. Cones of jack pines will release their seeds only after being scorched by a forest fire. Prairie grasses depend on lightning strikes to ignite fires and on grazing by herds of bison to stimulate their growth and keep other plant species from invading their habitat.

These ideas of constant change, complexity, and unpredictability are difficult enough to comprehend when applied to rocks, soils, rivers, plants, animals, and the myriad other facets of nature. But adding people to the equation creates new levels of complexity and vastly raises the stakes. Human beings have a long history of directly or indirectly nudging species over the brink, and David Quammen describes the swath our species has cut through the world's biodiversity as human populations spread to the far corners of the planet. The process has not stopped, and we may learn its costs too late to slow it.

Whatever successes we may have in reconciling our conceptions of nature with change and instability, the fact remains that people will still want to feed themselves on a regular basis, and will want to keep themselves, their loved ones, and their property out of harm's way. Fires, floods, and volcanoes all demonstrably contribute to sustaining the Earth and its ecosystems. But they also tend to conflict with the material interests of humans.

This is why it is especially important that discussions about how we should relate to nature in the future be opened up to as wide a range of voices as possible. George Horse Capture and Helena Norberg-Hodge write of two cultures, one in Montana and the other in the northern extreme of India, that made their peace with nature centuries ago, only to have it disrupted by outside forces. During the 1980s mining interests and the global demand for gold reached into Montana and onto the land of the A'aninin people, and, ploying machinery and explosives, took away something sacred—an entire mountain. High in the Indian sector of the Tibetan Plateau the mountains all remain in place, but beginning in the 1970s the Ladakhi people have had to struggle to preserve their cultural traditions and environmentally benign lifestyle against a rising tide of consumer culture and Western-style development schemes.

Edward Ayensu, writing of Africa, warns of something different. By ignoring or suppressing the indigenous knowledge and inventiveness of people in so-called developing countries, the world misses opportunities to harness skills for solving global problems, particularly in the areas of biodiversity and herbal medicine. Bringing in appropriate technology—better telecommunications systems, for instance—can stimulate this process without displacing traditional lifestyles.

To accommodate realities of nature and the needs and rights of diverse cultures around the world, we need to restructure political and economic decisions, making processes to accommodate nature's complex systems. Gretchen Daily suggests that to begin,

I wish to speak a word for Nature,
for absolute freedom and wildness.

—HENRY DAVID THOREAU

we need to identify the connections between natural ecosystems and our economic and political systems—especially those that provide economic or social benefits, or "ecosystems services." Insects pollinate crops for free, forests purify water, and the entire biosphere maintains a gigantic genetic library holding the codes for potential medicines, crops, fuels, and other valuable products.

Nature, in its unobtrusive way, has been bankrolling human societies for millennia; it is time we included its contributions in our economic calculations and decision making. And, if we are coming to understand that human beings have a place in nature, we must also grant that nature has an honored place in our society.

The Wilkes Expedition is remembered today as a seminal event in the development of American science. On returning home after four years of intensive scientific research, specimen collecting, and mapmaking, expedition members were greeted not by acclaim but by controversy and confusion. Their claims of sighting a new continent were not believed. Recriminations among the officers regarding disciplinary practices during the voyage led to a court-martial and public reprimand of Wilkes. Despite the clear scientific value of the expedition's extensive biological, geological, and ethnographic specimens, no branch or institution in the government had the resources to properly curate them. Instead, members of Congress and other influential figures raided the collections for souvenirs.

Thanks to the single-minded determination of Wilkes and his colleagues, the bulk of the expedition's collections and data remained intact. In 1857 the collections were turned over to the fledgling Smithsonian Institution to establish a National Museum of the United States. The collections formed the nucleus of what is now the National Museum of Natural History, where scientists, scholars, artists, and other specialists, working in the tradition of the Wilkes Expedition, continue to expand the frontiers of our understanding of nature. The frontiers are less well defined than they were 160 years ago, and they extend far beyond our planet into outer space, back in time to the origins of the universe and life, and to scales of size both much larger and much smaller than a person can genuinely comprehend.

To explore these new frontiers, we use tools that were not available to 19th-century explorers—spacecraft, electron microscopes, gene sequencers, computers—and bring with us ideas and perspectives that reflect the intervening century and a half of cultural change. But the basic challenge is the same: to respect and to understand as best we can the complex, shifting web of processes and interdependencies that we call nature.

Forest fires torched vast tracts of Yellowstone National Park
to blackened cinder, yet just a decade later, lush growth
carpets the former forest floor. The cycle of destruction and
regeneration replays throughout nature, from lava-carved
volcano slopes to spreading river floodplains.

PART ONE

Forces of Nature

Images from space show the Earth as a serene blue orb, with only the white swirls of clouds hinting at its dynamism. Our planet operates on scales much grander than the human brain is equipped to comprehend. The constant motion of the atmosphere and oceans is driven by the sun's energy; the slow but occasionally violent movement of the crust is driven by Earth's own heat. Understanding the Earth begins with understanding its physical systems, the natural forces that have made it hospitable to life and that continue to shape its evolution. As each of these essays suggests, it is no easy task.

Climate Surprises

JONATHAN OVERPECK

*Climate has been traditionally assumed to be both stable
and predictable, except when disrupted by unusual conditions.
But relict sand dunes, tree rings, and other records of past
climates show evidence of megadroughts and other climate
surprises over the past 2,000 years. Such events are likely
to recur without warning, so society must prepare to adapt.*

In the summer of 1998, withering heat and severe drought gripped the states of Texas and Oklahoma. By August, the President had declared all 254 counties in Texas federal disaster areas. The economic impact of the drought on the two states would ultimately approach $7 billion, leading to reports that the drought of 1998 was the nation's most severe since the 1930s.

But in 1988-89, only ten years before, a two-year drought had inflicted economic damage that totaled almost $40 billion. And, of course, still farther back in time was the drought of true legend: the Dust Bowl of the 1930s. Before it was over, the Dust Bowl drought affected most of the lower 48 states, stretching at its maximum (in 1934) from the Ohio River Valley to California and from Mexico to Canada. Temperatures exceeded 110°F in the central High Plains.

In contrast, the drought of 1998 mapped like a bull's-eye on the state of Texas, with a little spilling over into the adjacent states; temperatures barely sneaked into the low 100s. The total economic impact of the Dust Bowl drought has never been fully documented, but its drama and impact on the land and people were immortalized by John Steinbeck in his epic novel, *The Grapes of Wrath:*

> The sun flared down on the growing corn day after day until a line of brown spread along the edge of each green bayonet. The clouds appeared, and went away, and in a while they did not try any more…. In the roads where the teams moved, where the wheels milled the ground and the hooves of the horses beat the ground, the dirt crust broke and the dust formed. Every moving thing lifted the dust into the air: a walking man lifted a thin layer as high as his waist, and a wagon lifted the dust as high as the fence tops, and an automobile boiled a cloud behind it. The dust was long in settling back again.

The drought of the 1930s was different. What made it so unusual, and so devastating, was its duration: It spanned the entire decade. How many of us, when reading accounts of the 1998 drought, even momentarily considered what it would be like if such a drought were to last ten years? How many of Steinbeck's readers stopped to ponder the likelihood of another multiyear drought as

Ancient rock carvings of giraffes recall a distant, lush past in the Sahara.

bad—or worse—than the one that caused the Dust Bowl?

As we enter the 21st century, and record-breaking global temperatures, destructive storms, and other extremes of climate get more and more attention in the press, many people—scientists, policy makers, and others—are now starting to ask these kinds of questions. Global warming, the possibility of its human causes, and its potential consequences, have become high-profile environmental concerns. Moreover, El Niño, a formerly obscure climatic phenomenon, has become so ingrained in the public consciousness that advertisers use it to sell everything from new roofs to ski vacations. We've also heard about its more serious impacts around the world: the floods, mud slides, droughts, fires, and coral reef bleaching.

Gauging from all the reports, something must be going on with our climate. But it is hard for anyone, even specialists in the study of climate, to know just how much of this impression is due to our limited perspective and imperfect memories, and how much stems from genuine changes in the Earth's condition. After all, human populations worldwide continue to increase and crowd into regions that are susceptible to climatic extremes. Along the eastern U.S. seaboard, development has increasingly spread to parts of the coastline where it is more likely that hurricanes will threaten people, their homes, and, consequently, their pocketbooks. Similarly, as more and more people move to arid regions, like the western United States, the odds increase that they will be hit by droughts or floods. And our increasingly interconnected global economy means that we are more and more likely to feel the effects of climatic events anywhere in the world; a climate disaster in China, for example, may stifle the production of some goods and the demand for others, sending economic ripples throughout Asia and the rest of the world.

If we are going to anticipate future climate risks to society, we need to understand to what extent the risks are brought on by our own actions—adding greenhouse gases to the atmosphere or building communities in disaster-prone areas— and to what extent they arise from the purely natural rhythms of climate change. Most importantly, we must acknowledge that Mother Nature may have surprises in store for us as we move into and through this millennium. A big question being asked now by scientists is whether, in the short history of climate research, we have seen the full range of climate behavior that Mother Nature might throw at us someday. Are the archives of our instrumental and satellite measurements from the last 150 years long enough or complete enough to tell us whether droughts on the scale of the Dust Bowl are likely to recur? How often? Can we rule out the possibility of even longer droughts—20 years, 50 years, or more?

The answer to these questions is unequivocally no. One and a half centuries of data does not begin to give us enough information on the extremes of natural climate cycles. We need to extend our search for changing climates by looking back centuries and millennia. Of course this takes some detective work. Without an archive of measurement from thermometers, rain gauges, and other meteorological instruments to help us decipher past climates, we need to rely on other kinds of clues.

In some cases, past climate variations are stored away by biological processes. For example, year-to-year changes in temperature and rainfall can precisely determine how much a tree grew in

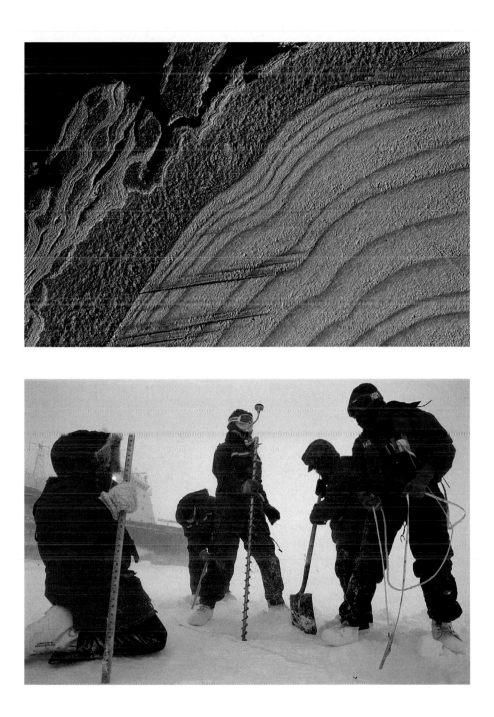

As accurate as any rain gauge, varying widths of tree growth rings (top) reveal wet and dry periods—in this case, four years of drought. Similarly, core samples taken of glacial Antarctic ice (bottom) tell of climate change long ago. Such samples may contain gases typical of Earth's atmosphere at a given time. And like tree rings, the thicknesses of periodic ice strata give information about precipitation levels.

Blowing sand from a dry lake bed clings to
Tinalbaraka walet Mohamed's eight month-old
daughter, Isha, as mother and children sleep on
a sun-baked afternoon in Mali. Just 25 years ago
lakes dotted the homeland of these nomadic
Tuareg people. The rains stopped in the 1970s,
but population growth and overgrazing did not.
"We used to fish, grow crops, have animals,
and prosper," says Tuareg leader Mohamed Ali.
"Now it is a country of thirst."

One never knows what will happen if things are suddenly changed.
But do we know what will happen if they are not changed?

— ELIAS CANETTI

a year. Since trees provide the opportunity to measure annual growth going back hundreds to thousands of years (for example, using tree-ring widths), we therefore are able to reconstruct both temperature and rainfall going back the same amount of time.

In other cases, such as with corals, the record of past climate change is locked up by chemical processes. The changing temperatures of seawater in which a coral is growing alters the chemistry of each seasonal band in the coral. Bands can be counted back for centuries and their chemical makeup sampled without harming the coral, making it possible to get a record of how sea surface temperatures varied from season to season and year to year long before anyone with a thermometer was around to do the job. Ice cores drilled from Antarctica and the Arctic and from high-mountain glaciers yield frozen records not only of past precipitation but also of the former atmosphere. Both the ice and ancient air bubbles trapped within it provide samples of airborne dust, greenhouse gases, and other climatically important constituents of the atmosphere. Lake and marine sediments piling up slowly on the lake or ocean bottom for hundreds and thousands of years contain an array of fossils and chemical indicators of what the local climate was like during the time they were being laid down. The list goes on. Modern paleoclimatologists now have a wide variety of natural archives and climate reconstruction methods at their disposal. The climate histories they have unraveled clearly indicate that the climate shifts and events of the last hundred years, including the recent shifts in El Niño and the range of severe droughts, are but a subset of what could confront human societies of the future.

In fact, I can see evidence of just such an ancient climate shift from the vantage of my aircraft window each time I fly in and out of Denver, as I often do for my work. To the east stretch the High Plains, one of the breadbaskets of our country. From the ground the plains present an unchanging view of cattle and farms, mile after mile. But from the air I see something that astounds me today, as it did when I first flew over the area in 1991. The flat, fertile plains are covered with the unmistakable shapes of forgotten, ancient sand dunes that once moved across a desertlike landscape.

I have been lucky enough to visit some of these ancient deposits with two of the researchers who know them best, Dan Muhs and Rich Madole of the U.S. Geological Survey. Dan and Rich, with their colleagues, have found that among the tens of thousands of square miles of windblown sand and dust covering the U.S. High Plains are dunes that were actively moving within just the last thousand years. It had been assumed that they were far older relics of the Ice Age, when the Earth's wind and weather patterns were substantially different from those of today. But one thousand years ago is comparatively recent. What is especially impressive is that these same dunes were not moving during the 1930s Dust Bowl, the worst drought recorded in U.S. history. What kind of drought could cause large areas of the High Plains to dry out into another Sahara?

We are now beginning to assemble a picture of these paleoclimatic events. Data from sources as diverse as the journals of early explorers, tree rings, lake sediments, river deposits, archaeological sites, and ancient dunes reveal what the instrument records cannot: Multiyear droughts similar to that of the 1930s tend to occur at a rate of one or two per century. More surprising, however, is the growing paleoclimatic evidence for

A sea of sand ripples across the Nebraska plains (above), remnants of towering Saharalike dunes that once dominated the region's landscape. Even the great midwestern Dust Bowl created by severe droughts and land abuse in the 1930s (below) did not produce any landforms remotely as permanent. The dry period that produced Nebraska's sand dunes was no ordinary drought—it must have been a major climatological variation.

megadroughts—droughts lasting for decades, rather than just years.

We now have good evidence that these truly extreme droughts have happened at a rate of two to three per thousand years, most recently during the 16th century, and that they affected much of North America. Not only did these megadroughts hit the High Plains, leaving the dunes and other windblown deposits there, but they also caused water sources in the Sierra Nevada and other western mountain ranges to go dry for decades at a time. The 16th-century drought even reached the Atlantic coast. Evidence from tree rings and historical journals suggests that this multiyear drought played a role in the disappearance of the earliest English settlement in North America, the so-called Lost Colony on Roanoke Island in North Carolina.

The devastating 1930s drought must have been a minor event compared to the megadrought that got the sand dunes moving on the High Plains a thousand years ago. What caused these multidecade droughts? We know only that they were caused by entirely natural processes—and that they could happen again without warning.

Learning how to predict and prepare for a possible megadrought will be a true challenge for the 21st century. We need to understand that all aspects of our climate are subject to change. There is no reason to expect that the average, or normal, climate of the next 30 years will be the same as that of the last 30 years. Because effective weather prediction is limited to four, five, maybe six days ahead, we generally rely on what has in the past been normal weather to anticipate and plan for what we think lies ahead. Many social and economic decisions are based on the assumption that the climate of the next year, next decade, and even next century will be much the same as

that of the last 30 to 150 years. But continuing this way could become a costly mistake, particularly in the new millennium, because we now know that climates are always changing. What we call normal climates are just snapshots along the way.

A new "climates-of-change" paradigm is emerging in climatology, based on a wide variety of climate observations—some observations, such as those of the dunes of the High Plains, cite changes hundreds and thousands of years in the past. We are learning how droughts and other local climate events fit into larger, more global phenomena, such as the current poster child of climate research, El Niño. During 1997 and 1998 a strong El Niño event affected much of the Earth. In the tropical Pacific heart of El Niño, the event was clearly underway when surface winds reversed their usual orientation and began to push warmer-than-normal surface water into the eastern tropical Pacific. With the eastward shift of the warm water came heavy rains, drenching the region and leaving behind anomalous dry conditions in the western tropical Pacific. These changes meant devastating rains, snowfalls, floods, and mud slides for the west coast of South and North America, major drought and forest fires for Papua New Guinea and Indonesia. Week after week, newspapers and televisions told of El Niño's effects around the world and resulting economic losses that soared into the billions of dollars.

But there is also a hopeful side to the El Niño story. The 1997-98 El Niño marked the beginning of a new era in our ability to predict climate: For the first time in human history, scientists and decision makers were able to anticipate and plan for El Niño's devastating effects, saving lives, property, and money. But despite this success, climate researchers are well aware that our understanding of El Niño and our predictive abilities are still very limited. In 1976 there was an abrupt and poorly understood warming across much of the Pacific that persists to this day. This warming in turn set the stage for the two strongest El Niños ever known. Additionally, before 1990, each El Niño tended to last just one or two years. But after 1990, we were surprised by an event that lasted five years. And with these abrupt shifts in El Niño's behavior have come shifts in its impacts around the globe—reminders that climate can change in many ways that we still don't understand.

One of the most astounding contributions to the climate revolution has come from even further back in time than the megadroughts of the High Plains. This was the discovery of extraordinarily abrupt "climate surprises" (as called by Wally Broecker of Columbia University) during the last glacial period, from 10,000 to 100,000 years ago. This was the Ice Age, when massive ice sheets covered most of northern North America and Europe, and the vegetation belts and ocean currents around the world were markedly different from today. Decades ago, paleoclimatologists had

found that these great ice ages were quasiperiodic phenomena—cold glacial periods and warm interglacial periods alternated approximately every 100,000 years. Further evidence indicated that subtle changes in the Earth's orbit around the sun served as the pacemaker for these cycles. This orbital theory dominated climate-change thinking for many years, along with the underlying assumption that gradual changes in the variables controlling climate change, such as slow shifts in Earth's orbit, would cause similarly gradual changes in climate, such as the coming and going of ice ages over many thousands of years.

About ten years ago, though, new pieces of the ice age puzzle were discovered that didn't seem to fit this model. Paleoclimatologists studying an array of ice cores from Greenland and sediment cores from the North Atlantic began to uncover evidence that the ice ages were not simply long, slowly changing, cold periods. They were shot through with abrupt periods of ice sheet collapse and regional climatic warming. What really caught the attention of climate scientists was the observation that many of these abrupt events— including regional increases in annual average temperatures of more than 15°F—happened over mere decades, or even years. The paradigm of gradually changing or stable climates began to fade. In its place came a new realization: Rather than shifting smoothly from one set of conditions to another, the world's climate systems tend to change abruptly, flip-flopping between stable states and spending little time in transition. Climate surprises appear to be the rule, rather than the exception, of climate change.

The consequences of a similar climate jump would be devastating for our society, but, luckily for us, the chances of such an event in the near future are probably not large. Most theories advanced to explain ice age climate surprises assume glacial ice sheets far larger than the Earth has today. The ice caps of Antarctica and Greenland probably aren't big or unstable enough to generate an ice age–scale climate surprise.

Does this mean that society is more or less free from the threat of climatic surprises in the future? Not at all. A whole new body of paleoclimatic evidence is emerging to suggest that warm climate surprises (as opposed to surprises during the cold ice ages) are much more common than previously thought. Add to this the fact that we are living in a warm interglacial period (not an ice age), and the implication is that warm climate surprises in the form of extreme droughts or higher frequencies of damaging hurricanes may be the most significant climatic threat worldwide in the 21st century. A surprise megadrought lasting a decade or more could wreak havoc on our country. Even in the absence of any global warming, it is possible that a future drought could start like the Texas-Oklahoma drought of 1998 and end up lasting for years, or even decades. It's hard to imagine the impact such a drought would have on our current economy, health, and lifestyle.

There are other reasons not to be complacent about future climate change. Over the last 150 years, the Earth has warmed significantly—by almost 1.5°F—and paleoclimatic records suggest this warming is the most dramatic in at least the last thousand years. Most climate scientists believe that some of this recent global warming is due to human-caused injections of greenhouse gases into the atmosphere, but it could be that some of the warming has natural roots as well. The greenhouse warming debate centers mostly on how big future human-induced climate changes will be. However, it might make sense for us all to recognize that climate change is what Mother Nature is all about, and that the most important 21st-century challenge is to develop the tools for predicting the full range of future climate change, whether driven by natural causes, human causes, or both.

Back in the 1930s, the United States was relatively empty and undeveloped compared to today. As I write, economic growth and development are booming across much of the country, and people continue to move into the regions that are perhaps most vulnerable to climates of change. As this happens, our economy is also becoming more and more intertwined with the economies of other countries around the world, each faced with responding to the changes in its own climate. To keep our economies strong—and, more important, to save lives and property—society and scientists alike need to perceive climate change as a natural, as well as a human-induced, phenomenon. We still have much to learn from the climates of the past, but our biggest challenge will be to use this growing body of knowledge to develop both the scientific and the social tools needed to anticipate and thrive as we face the changing climates to come.

The Changing Landscape of Knowledge

BERNICE WUETHRICH

In the dry southeast of Madagascar, a eucalyptus-lined road crests a hill that is studded with triangle palms *(Dypsis decaryi)*. Local people call the tree *lafa*. It is a rare plant that grows nowhere else in the world but on this island. Hill and palm belong to the Andohahela nature reserve—one of Madagascar's largest. Although local people long used lafa wood to build their houses, fronds to shield the sun, and fruit to feed their children, the palm has been officially protected, so to speak, since 1939, when the French colonial government created the reserve.

During colonial rule, a labor camp operated next to the hill. Tatsimo men were among those forced to build the road and plant the eucalyptus that marks the nature reserve. Before the reserve existed, villagers followed a footpath around the hill to a central market. The path led to other landscapes as well—a spiny forest of thorned plants, where *helos,* or spirits, resided in stones and trees. The land still brims with spiritual and material resources, but the well-trodden path is severed at the edge of the Andohahela reserve, which remains strictly off-limits. Therefore, when a Tatsimo villager views the eucalyptus, the hill, and the palms, he may see something very different from what a biologist bent on conserving rare species sees.

"Whether you understand it or not, there is always history in the landscape," says anthropologist Wendy Walker. That history is social, cultural, biological—and it is ever evolving. "We need to move beyond thinking about a particular area simply as a place to save or as a source of biodiversity. There are very intricate ways in which local people relate to their landscapes." Walker, who spent two years in Madagascar, learning about Tatsimo concepts of nature, urges an expansive view of the meaning of biodiversity—and ways of thinking that may differ radically from those of biological science.

Fortunately, more and more conservationists are recognizing the value of local knowledge and engaging in dialogue with groups such as Madagascar's Tatsimo. Some researchers are collaborating with indigenous populations to identify and conserve plants likely to contain medicinal compounds, searching for cures for cancer, AIDS, and dozens of ailments. The hope is that sharing knowledge will lead not only to new medicines but also to better conservation, increased economic opportunities, and possibly whole new paradigms for the treatment of disease.

The desire to harvest the world's plant pharmacopoeia is undoubtedly as old as our species. Some of the earliest written records document such efforts. Script on Egyptian papyrus from 1550 B.C. refers to the use of tree oils to repel mosquitoes as protection against a disease now thought to have been malaria. Of today's drugs, almost half have an origin in natural products. Renowned among them are alkaloids produced by the rosy periwinkle, a flowering shrub native to Madagascar. Doctors prescribe its chemical compounds to treat childhood leukemia and Hodgkin's disease. Quinine, the first antimalarial drug known to Western medicine, comes from the bark of cinchona trees. Jesuit missionaries learned of its curative properties from native people in the Peruvian highlands and introduced the drug to Europe about 1640. It is still in use.

Walter Lewis, a biologist at Washington University in St. Louis, Missouri, and his team have collected promising plant species in the Andean foothills of Peru and adjacent Amazon basin since 1982. They worked with a linguistic anthropologist and gradually built strong ties with the Aguaruna and Achuar tribes of the Jivaro people. Over generations, these forest-dwelling people had become intimately familiar with the region's abundant flora, and developed a medical practice utilizing some 500 of the region's 10,000 plant species.

Lewis is keenly interested in Aguaruna treatment of malaria. Some strains have developed resistance to most standard drugs—including quinine—and each year the disease kills about two million people worldwide. Pregnant women and their fetuses are especially vulnerable. After years of joint work—and signing contracts that assure future benefit sharing with Peruvian universities and indigenous clans —Aguaruna medical practitioners led Lewis to some ten antimalarial plants. They instructed Lewis on the plants' harvest and preparation. Back in his lab, Lewis isolated plant compounds that kill the parasite in human red blood cells. "Without the collaboration of the indigenous people who are partners, we'd be nowhere," Lewis says candidly. His project is part of the International Cooperative Biodiversity Groups

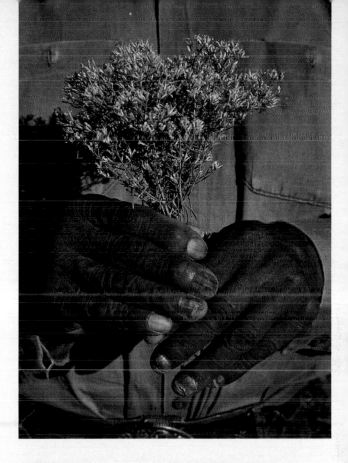

Snakeweed—here held by a rancher/medicine man in Arizona's Sonoran Desert—may hold a treatment for arthritis. Scientists are scattering worldwide, racing the environmental clock to assess traditional therapies using various plant species—some of which may be endangered.

program, which promotes cross-cultural collaboration in the process of drug discovery. The aim is to improve human health, encourage conservation, and provide local economic benefits.

So that their Aguaruna partners realize benefits from conservation efforts, Lewis's team helped them develop nurseries to grow medicinal plants—several types of which have become scarce in the wild. The concept of conservation is relatively new to the Aguaruna. As seminomadic people, they moved their villages about every ten years, a practice that allowed previously occupied land to rebound from clearing and harvesting. In the 1970s the Aguaruna villages became permanent. This change in lifestyle called for a change in thinking, since a sedentary population can quickly denude the surrounding area of wild resources. Now the Aguaruna cultivate medicinal plants on hundreds of hectares, some in secondary forest, others interspersed in their original settings.

The landscape of the Andean foothills is changing as villages expand and as people attend to old resources in new ways. The landscape of knowledge is also transforming, for the Aguaruna people and the international team of biologists working with them. This union of two knowledge systems, both born of astute observation and experimentation, is not only sowing fertile ground for new medical practices, but also cultivating a cross-cultural dialogue that promises profound rewards.

Streams of Consciousness

ALAN CUTLER

Water is the essence of life on Earth and flowing water the primary sculptor of the Earth's surface. Human society has had a long and intimate relationship with rivers and streams, complicated by their variability and unpredictability—and even more by our clumsy insistence on trying to control them.

In 1959 Little Falls Branch, a minor tributary of the Potomac River just outside of Washington, D.C., caught fire. The watershed of Little Falls Branch was no polluted industrial wasteland; it was residential, with comfortable neighborhoods that were home to diplomats, professionals, and government officials.

The creek had been contaminated by an oil spill, which then ignited. The fire burned for two days, its heat so intense that the Massachusetts Avenue bridge across the creek melted, shutting down a major route into the city. Commuters, most of whom had probably never noticed the creek, had to find other ways to get to their jobs at embassies and federal agencies. The fire thrust the obscure watercourse into a role usually reserved for larger bodies of water: It was a geographical barrier, an impediment (albeit minor) to the affairs of great nations.

I grew up along a nearby creek, Minnehaha Branch, in suburban Maryland. That creek did not have to burst into flames to capture my attention. It just had to be there, with its pools and riffles to wade through, rocks to flip over, and banks to dig into. My brother and I built dams

across its channel, and then watched the water rise, spill over the sand embankments, and sweep the dam away. We scooped up tadpoles and frogs' eggs in mayonnaise jars. We sifted through the sand and gravel for gold, finding instead glittering flakes of mica and particles of black iron oxide (with a magnet, you could collect it by the jarful). We raced floating leaves through the riffles and watched sand grains on the bottom creep downstream with the current, some pausing in a hollow or on a bar, others tumbling steadily along or wafting upward on the occasional eddy. The creek offered unlimited possibilities for a young naturalist.

For sheer excitement, nothing rivaled the floods. After a heavy rain, the creek filled nearly to the tops of its banks, becoming a swift and fearsome torrent. Great waves of rushing brown water would rear up and froth where earlier we had stalked crayfish or skipped pebbles. It was an inspiring sight. Standing on the slippery banks, we heaved logs into the current, watching them disappear downstream with the other flotsam. The creek's flash floods—the way they transformed the placid Minnehaha Branch into

Wise water management begins where rivers begin—upstream in bubbling waters like Michigan's Sturgeon River Gorge.

The universe is full of magical things patiently waiting for our wits to grow sharper.

—EDEN PHILLPOTTS

a mighty Colorado—awed me as few natural spectacles have since.

But the Minnehaha floods were no more natural than the flames of Little Falls Branch. They were the unruly consequence of how utterly the landscape had been transformed. Before we built our houses and paved our streets, the land around the Minnehaha, its soil and vegetation, had soaked up most of the rain as it fell. The water then made its way to the stream, not so much flowing as oozing, making stops along the way to replenish a root or leach some bedrock. Because the flow to the creek was slowed and buffered by the intervening sponge of plants and soil, the Minnehaha Branch would have maintained a fairly steady flow, its moderate fluctuations tied to the seasonal changes in precipitation.

But when our houses went up, their roofs shedding water, and our streets and driveways got paved so that our vehicles would not churn the ground into mud, the rainwater began to bypass the natural buffering system, moving directly from pavement to gutter to storm sewer to creek, the neighborhood runoff swiftly converging at more or less the same time on the creek's narrow channel. And so the water shot through it as if from a fire hose. It was a great show for the kids—but it was not the way a woodland stream was supposed to work.

Nothing on Earth is so mysterious as water. Throughout history we have built settlements along watercourses, used rivers and river valleys as routes of commerce and exploration, and availed ourselves of river water to irrigate crops and flush wastes. As symbol and metaphor, water is a staple of world mythology, religion, and literature. It falls out of the sky and flows downhill. It puts out fires and makes plants grow. Turn on the faucet and there it is.

But water poses a problem, too. Scientists, policy makers, and environmentalists tell us that, of the societal and environmental issues looming as the major challenges of the next century, the most formidable will involve water—fresh water for agriculture (crop irrigation is by far the biggest consumer of water), clean water for human health (each year water-related diseases claim the lives of more than five million people worldwide), and the preservation of wetlands and clean rivers for the vast number of plant and animal species that depend on them. More and more, human populations are crowding into arid regions, putting impossible demands on the meager water resources. Climate change, driven by human activities and natural cycles, seems likely to beset us with ever more extreme droughts, floods, and violent storms.

Water, or lack of it, is often what defines a natural environment. Whether the water flows, whether it freezes or stays liquid year-round, whether it is fresh or salty, whether it falls from the clouds in the summer or winter—all these factors dictate the type of wildlife present and how humans must interact with the environment if it is to continue to thrive. Yet this familiar and renewable resource confounds our best attempts to understand and manage it.

Water is an almost universal solvent; practically anything from minerals to elaborate organic compounds will dissolve in it to some degree. This makes water the perfect medium for complex biochemical reactions involving many kinds of molecules, and therefore the perfect liquid base for the sap of a living cell. All life functions are based on chemical reactions, which is why plants, humans, and other organisms are so completely

Living by rivers for many millennia, people have had to adapt to the extreme cycles of their flows. Periodic flooding in Cambodia's Mekong Delta was the worst in memory in 1991 (above). The river rose 25 feet, and thousands of acres of paddy fields were ruined. Traditional stilt houses proved equal to the threat. Four months later (left), the waters had retreated and crops were growing in the fertile, silty soil left behind by the floods.

dependent on water. A dehydrated cell is a dead cell. But water's chemistry is also its curse: All manner of toxins, carcinogens, and other bizarre creations of industrial chemistry are also readily dissolved in water, making it easy for them to contaminate water supplies and spread through ecosystems. Water is just as efficient a medium for conveying harmful substances as it is for conveying beneficial ones.

Water's molecular properties have their effects on grander scales, too. The volatility of weather and the violence of storms owe their origin to the simple process by which water enters the atmosphere: evaporation. When water is in a liquid state, its individual molecules easily jostle and move past one another; water flows. But the molecules are not completely independent of one another. They form temporary bonds called hydrogen bonds, which have to be broken for the liquid to turn into gas—and that takes energy.

A lot of energy. To evaporate any quantity of water—a drop—requires 540 times as much heat energy as it does to raise the temperature of that same water 1°C. This property of water, known as the latent heat of vaporization, explains why climbing out of a cold swimming pool into the hot sun can be an uncomfortably chilly experience. The thin film of water evaporating from the surface of your skin sucks heat from your body faster than the frigid pool water could. And this heat energy, like all energy, is conserved, and where the water vapor goes, it goes too.

If the vapor rises into the atmosphere and cools enough for it to condense back into a drop of water, the heat energy is released into the surrounding air. The air stays warm and so keeps on rising, causing more water vapor to condense, releasing still more heat, causing the air to rise still farther, causing more condensation, and on and on in an accelerating updraft. The rising column of air sucks other moisture-laden air up behind it, feeding and perpetuating the process. On a hot summer afternoon, the result can be a thunderhead, which may put on a show of wind and lightning before dumping its water back onto the ground in a cloudburst. Hurricanes get their phenomenal destructive power from the latent heat absorbed during the evaporation of tropical seawater. The water is not even lukewarm—usually 80 degrees compared to our bodies' 98.6°F—but when the latent heat from thousands of square miles is concentrated into a single vortex, wind speeds can exceed 200 miles per hour, and the total energy released by the storm can match that of 400 20-megaton nuclear explosions. Water vapor, with its transitions to and from liquid water, keeps the atmosphere stirred up and makes the weather hard to predict.

This constant traffic of water in and out of the atmosphere, rising from the sea, falling on the hills and plains, soaking and scouring the solid earth, also shapes the landscape. Water is by far the most potent agent of erosion on the planet. The hills, ridges, and pinnacles of any given topography are generally the product of terrain worn down by the relentless action of water and ice. A prominence may stand in relief because its bedrock was particularly hard and unerodible, or because the channel of a primordial

stream happened to twist one way instead of another, sparing the patch of ground from the brunt of erosion and down-cutting in the deepening stream valley.

Every geologic cataclysm or upheaval of rock and magma is ultimately tamed and defeated by water. There are few places on Earth where you can set your feet and not be standing on the corpse of a mountain range or volcano that had its peaks torn apart by ice and its flanks beveled by rain and snowmelt. Mountains raised in haste by plate tectonics will be flattened at leisure by erosion. There is more of the Appalachian Mountain chain lying pulverized off the Atlantic coast of North America than there is in the present-day mountain ridges. Walking along the Potomac River, it's easy to find pebbles of the same bedrock that many miles to the west holds up the ridges and crags of Appalachia. The pebbles, rounded from their journey thus far, are headed for the sea. The rest of the mountain rock will eventually follow them, though not in my lifetime, or even necessarily in the lifetime of our species.

Despite its preeminence as a force of erosion, it would be a mistake to think of flowing water simply in terms of destruction. Water is also a force of renewal. Without the breakup and dissolution of rocks by the water that rains down over the continents, life on Earth, if it did not cease altogether, would become minimally productive. The erosion cycle is a nutrient mill in which the rocks of the Earth's crust are ground into plant and plankton food and then washed downhill to the soils and waters of terrestrial and, ultimately, marine ecosystems. If erosion and weathering weren't constantly releasing fresh supplies of calcium, sodium, and other critical nutrients from the land's underlying rocks, the biosphere would

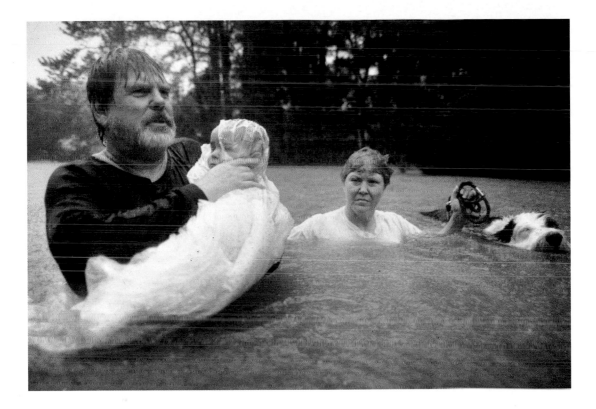

As flood waters rise in Conroe, Texas, a couple who had been babysitting their grandchild struggle to safety. Torrential downpours in the fall of 1994 flooded vast areas of southern Texas. Along the San Jacinto River some 10,000 people were forced from their homes. Near the river's mouth in Houston, the natural disaster spawned a man-made one when pipelines failed and gasoline, crude oil, heating oil, and natural gas poured out and ignited in a firestorm that engulfed woods, houses, boats, and barges.

A simple assessment of a river's floodplain ought to alert people to their chances of periodic inundation, yet development pushes ever closer to the coastline and vulnerable waterfronts. Attempting to solve the dilemma, dams can be built either to block overflow at a river's banks or to divert the flow completely.

Holding back the flow of one of America's largest rivers, 726-foot-high Hoover Dam (right), in operation since 1935, domesticated the Colorado, whose floods once tore through the countryside. Still, such progress comes with a price: Hundreds of miles downstream, the Colorado now virtually disappears before reaching the sea, its waters diverted for human use.

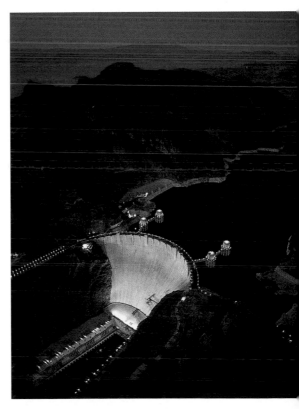

In the Grand Canyon, slow but persistent waters from Deer Creek etch away at the Tapeats sandstone at a rate of roughly one inch per century. The sandstone itself was deposited 500 million years ago, when long-vanished rivers carried sand into an ancient sea.

ultimately wind down, because even the most efficient ecosystem's nutrient cycles always spill a little "downstream," with the ultimate nutrient sink being the oceanic abyss.

Standing at a river's edge or on the banks of a creek, what we see is not really where the system begins or ends. The real river extends far beyond the margins of its channel; it includes the whole of its watershed, the total extent of land on which its water collects and drains, including the subsurface, which can feed the stream by seepage from groundwater. The river is part of the great hydrologic cycle that connects the atmosphere with the oceans, with many detours through the biosphere and lithosphere. The river is far more than just its water. It is also the flotsam bobbing on its surface, the cobbles and boulders rolling downstream during its floods, the sand, silt, clay, and gravel entrained by its currents, the chemicals and minerals dissolved in its water. It is the floodplain, the gravel bars, the meanders, and the oxbows. It is also the plants, animals, fungi, and bacteria living not only within its channel but within its entire catchment. All are as much a part of the river system as any eddy or riffle—and not in a metaphorical sense, either. Chop down too many trees in the watershed, or build your house on the floodplain, and when the next hurricane roars in from the coast to drop its load of rain, the connections will become very clear.

For centuries people have made the obvious comparison between the Earth's network of rivers and the human body's circulatory system: Each carries through its branching channels the primary liquid for sustaining its life. Perhaps a better analogy was proposed in 1994 by Luna Leopold, one of the 20th century's influential and insightful students of rivers, who is now professor emeritus at the University of California at Berkeley. Leopold suggested that, in their complexity, development, and behavior, rivers resemble nothing so much as an evolving biological species. River and stream channels, regardless of size, show an amazing consistency in their geometric shapes—meander bends, for example, develop according to well-defined mathematical relationships. But like individuals within a species, each river system is unique, its individual pattern as recognizable as a human face. And in both rivers and species the complexity and integration of parts arise not from a fixed or predetermined plan but rather from the interplay between chance, history, and deterministic physical law. Both have histories, and each changes and adapts to changing conditions. The result is an idiosyncratic and changeable entity that defies generalization and, as Leopold remarked, "has a heritage, but no beginning."

Before his death, in 1948, Aldo Leopold, Luna's father and a prescient thinker about the environment, wrote an essay on the lumberjack Paul Bunyan and Wisconsin's fabled Round River. Round River, the story went, had no beginning or end. Its channel formed a closed loop, perpet-ually flowing into itself. Bunyan and his team of loggers discovered the miraculous river while on a lumber drive: After floating their logs for miles on the swift current they were startled to realize that it was carrying them around and around, always through the same territory.

Leopold saw in the story of Round River a parable of nature and of our species' perpetually unsettled relationship with it. Too often we don't acknowledge that when we tamper with natural systems—a watershed or an ecosystem, for

Rank and lifeless by the 1960s, this length of the Nashua River in Massachusetts (above, left) was a toxic stew of untreated sewage, running red with dye from paper mills. Today (above, right) it is a haven for anglers and canoeists and a model for communities striving to clean the waters they have fouled.

The river's death-and-rebirth saga began back in the 1960s, at what seemed a hopeless point in the history of North American water. Lake Erie was said to be on its deathbed. In Cleveland, Ohio, the Cuyahoga River caught fire. And the Nashua was one of the most blighted rivers in America, polluted to such an extent that its fumes blackened paint on nearby buildings.

Groton, Massachusetts, resident Marion Stoddart started a campaign to restore the Nashua and its tributaries. She built coalitions with business people, labor leadership, and paper companies, the worst polluters. Within a few years, people had cleaned up their businesses, changed state laws, and testified before Congress. With federal help, eight treatment plants were built or upgraded, and a broad conservation greenway was created along about half of the Nashua and two major tributaries. Today most of the industry is still there—and many parts of the river are safe for swimming.

Fall sets maple and birch aflame along the east branch of Michigan's Fox River. The meandering stream wanders across its flood plain, and scars of former channels are visible in the lower growth near the river's banks.

instance—the consequences have a way of looping back on us and catching us by surprise. The path that nature favors is not necessarily the straightforward, linear one we would expect.

"We of the genus *Homo* ride the logs that float down Round River," Aldo Leopold wrote, "and by a little judicious 'burling' we have learned to guide their direction and speed." By "burling" he meant trimming and smoothing the knots and irregularities of the logs. We try to control the things in nature that keep our civilization afloat; we straighten them out where we can; we do our best to direct their courses downstream, rather than take chances with the current.

Leopold saw the process as inadequate. "We burl our logs with more energy than skill," he observed. To preserve the functioning of a natural system, we need to learn ways of dealing with it besides hacking off the parts we don't understand or don't think we need. And all the burling in the world won't change the system's fundamental nature—it will curve, loop, and connect according to its own logic:

> Hydrologists have demonstrated that the meanderings of a creek are a necessary part of the hydrologic functioning. The flood plain belongs to the river. The ecologist sees clearly that for similar reasons we can get along with less channel improvement on Round River.

Now, a half century after Aldo Leopold spun his tale about real, mythical, and metaphorical rivers, we are thinking about them less simplistically. The problems are not getting simpler, of course, and at times our rate of progress can seem maddeningly slow, but we have become more aware of the consequences of tampering with these systems.

I now live along the Muddy Branch, also a tributary of the Potomac. The creek is flanked on both sides by a buffer zone of woods, as has been required by the local building code since the 1970s. An artificial holding pond collects much of the neighborhood runoff, slowing its rush to Muddy Branch and, as a bonus, providing habitat for herons, frogs, and dragonflies.

After a rain, Muddy Branch gushes more than it should—there are some heavily built-up areas upstream—but for a suburban creek, it is doing fine. A recent biological survey found 36 species of fish living in its waters. Even Little Falls Branch has shown some improvement: Though a 1976 study found it completely lifeless, more recent investigations have turned up a handful of pollution-tolerant fish and insect species.

Sadly, the Minnehaha Branch of my childhood explorations did not survive the 1960s. Its floods and erratic flow eventually became so problematic that, in an act suggesting some sort of euthanasia for creeks, the county encased it in a concrete pipe and buried it. Now it lies beneath a narrow, grassy swath that winds through the neighborhood, emerging a mile or so downstream.

But despite what the engineers and bulldozers did some 30 years ago, the contours of the land dictate that a creek should still be there. So sometimes, when I'm back in my old haunts, I check on the progress of a muddy little rivulet that forms after a rainstorm, which has cut a small channel through the turf. Here and there people have tried to save the grass by filling the shallow gully with rocks and sticks. It's a neighborhood of intelligent, accomplished, and professional people, but they don't understand. When it rains, the water just swirls around the obstacles and keeps digging.

The Force of City Life on Earth

BARBARA BOYLE TORREY

For thousands of years, as human populations grew, people spread around the globe, settling the land and clearing it for agriculture. But in the past 200 years, as the world's population has doubled and tripled, a different but equally potent kind of human migration has been taking place. For the first time in human history, nearly half of the world's population lives in urban areas.

The shift to cities is irrevocable. From now on, almost all future population growth will be in cities and towns. In the next 30 years, the number of people living in urban areas is expected to double. This fundamental change in where people live will affect human systems, such as economies, and natural systems, such as air and water, because urban people have quite different impacts on the world than rural people.

Urban populations have distinct consumption patterns, not only in wealthy, industrialized countries but also in developing countries around the world. In China during the 1970s, urban populations consumed more than twice the amount of pork that rural populations did, even though rural farmers were raising the pigs. As economic development progressed, rural diets improved in China, but even in the 1980s, the urban populations ate 60 percent more pork than the rural populations did. Urban dwellers also use more durable goods. In the early 1990s, households in urban areas of China were twice as likely to have a television and 25 times more likely to have a refrigerator than rural households.

Land-use patterns also differ. Most cities were not formally planned but sprang up where there were advantages in the local environment. Many cities evolved where transportation was easy, along rivers or coastal areas, such as New York and Tianjin, China. Others, such as Charlotte, North Carolina, and New Delhi, India, developed close to agriculture, to feed their nonfarming populations. Recent dramatic population increases affect land-use patterns far beyond the original borders of many cities, though. Delhi, India, was founded on good agricultural land next to the Yamuna River, but its urban sprawl engulfed many agricultural villages, removing farm land almost irreversibly.

Cities alter the natural flow of water by replacing porous agricultural soils with nonporous paved surfaces. Land that is impervious to rain is susceptible to flooding, and the size and frequency of floods increase as more land is paved. With flooding may come overflow of sewage systems, leading to pollution in the urban area and beyond. Coastal pollution in Brazil, for example, increased as untreated sewage from rapidly growing Sao Paulo overwhelmed waste treatment facilities and flowed into the three most important rivers serving the metropolitan region.

More energy is used for transportation, cooking, heating, and household appliances in urban areas, with a variety of consequences. In China air quality worsened as the urban consumption of coal grew to three times that in rural areas. In Jakarta, the use of wood for cooking and heating has led to major deforestation around the city. Recently, Jakartans changed from wood to kerosene and gas, trading deforestation for increased carbon dioxide emissions into the atmosphere.

As cities use energy, they generate heat. They also absorb more heat from the sun than agricultural lands, since buildings and pavement change the local albedo—the ability of a surface to reflect heat from the sun. As urban landscapes absorb heat from the sun, they become heat islands. New York City, for example, is estimated to be 1.1° C warmer than adjoining rural areas. Warmer cities can

Environmental impact depends on both the numbers of people and where they live. As the world's population grows, it is increasingly concentrated in cities, alleviating some enviromental problems but worsening others.

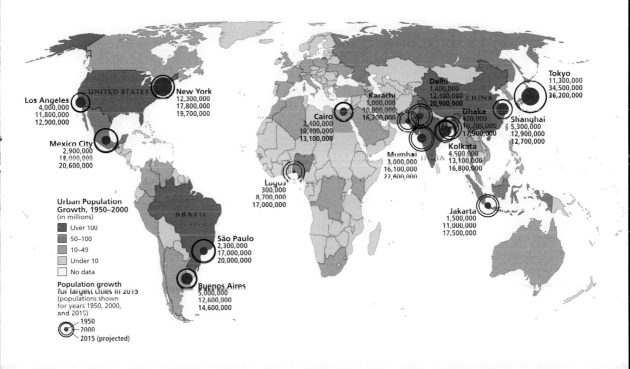

Los Angeles
4,000,000
11,800,000
12,900,000

New York
12,300,000
17,800,000
19,700,000

Mexico City
2,900,000
18,000,000
20,600,000

Cairo
2,400,000
10,400,000
13,100,000

Karachi
1,000,000
10,000,000
16,200,000

Delhi
1,400,000
12,400,000
20,900,000

Dhaka
400,000
10,200,000
17,900,000

Tokyo
11,300,000
34,500,000
36,200,000

Shanghai
5,300,000
12,900,000
12,700,000

Mumbai
3,000,000
16,100,000
22,600,000

Kolkata
4,500,000
13,100,000
16,800,000

Lagos
300,000
8,700,000
17,000,000

Jakarta
1,500,000
11,000,000
17,500,000

São Paulo
2,300,000
17,000,000
20,000,000

Buenos Aires
5,000,000
12,600,000
14,600,000

Urban Population Growth, 1950–2000
(in millions)

- Over 100
- 50–100
- 10–49
- Under 10
- No data

Population growth for largest cities in 2015
(populations shown for years 1950, 2000, and 2015)

- 1950
- 2000
- 2015 (projected)

affect local and regional weather patterns, increasing rain and fog and decreasing snowfall. Urban heat islands also tend to trap atmospheric particles, adding to air pollution.

The continued transition in the Earth's population from a rural to an urban concentration is likely to be a major force of change in the 21st century, and devising ways to lessen the impact of city dwelling on the natural world will put considerable demands on human ingenuity. Remote sensing by satellites can help monitor changes in urban expansion and project future growth. Pollution control technology can improve air quality dramatically, as it already has in Los Angeles and London. Management of water supplies is also becoming more efficient. All these technologies, however, require money. Not surprisingly, many of them are being used in wealthy industrialized countries but not yet in developing nations.

Creating an ecological city requires more than funding, however. It requires a strong sense of civic consciousness and responsibility. Civic, or social, capital is perhaps as important as money. If we are to adapt successfully and sustainably to a new, more urbanized world, we need to learn much more than we know today about the intended and unintended forces that cities unleash on the natural world. Then we can marshal the resources needed to act on that knowledge.

Global Synergies

WILLIAM MELSON

The rocky crust and underlying mantle are not merely the solid foundations for the dynamic systems of our planet; they are active participants. Powered by heat welling up from the Earth's interior, volcanic eruptions and geological upheavals have been major forces behind the evolution of the atmosphere, the oceans, and life's diversity.

For many people, the phrase "global change" brings to mind human impacts on the environment, especially warming climates and the extinction of species. Human activities have indeed changed the environment in many ways, and there is good reason to be concerned about human-mediated change in the future. But change is as old as the Earth. At times in the past 4.6 billion years, the Earth's climates have been both far warmer and far colder than the present. And the Earth has undergone, and rebounded from, at least five major extinction events. When we think about global change, we must consider the Earth as a system that has changed because of interactions among its parts—the atmosphere, ocean currents, the Earth's dynamic interior, and living organisms.

In the past 40 years, our understanding of the Earth's dynamic interior has taught us that its internal forces affect everything from climate to life. Yet we rarely appreciate that the geological forces that originate inside the Earth are fundamental to our planet's capacity to support life.

All life exists in a thin layer embedded between two vast heat engines. One engine, which heats the Earth's oceans, atmosphere, and land, is driven by energy from the sun. The other engine is fueled by the Earth's internal heat, which results mainly from the slow decay of radioactive elements such as uranium and thorium. Although these elements are present in the Earth's rocks at only trace levels (a few parts per million), they produce the energy that powers two of the Earth's major forces of change: plate tectonics and volcanism.

Plate tectonics is the slow motion of the Earth's relatively thin rocky layer, or lithosphere, that underlies continents and ocean basins. The lithosphere moves because of gigantic convection currents that are produced by the Earth's internal heat engine in the mantle. The mantle is a hot, denser layer of semisolid rock that lies between the lithosphere and the core. In the mantle, masses of hot rock rise and then sink as they cool, much as water in a boiling pot rises from the bottom as it heats and then descends along the pot's walls as it cools. This process of convection also breaks the lithosphere into fragments, or plates, that slowly move apart or move together, changing the structure of the Earth's surface. And as the number, size, and latitudes of

Still adding to Earth's atmosphere, a Guatemalan volcano ejects gases skyward.

Everything changes, nothing remains without change.

—BUDDHA

continents and ocean basins shift over geological time, the evolution and diversity of life responds.

Many of the discoveries that led to the theory of plate tectonics were made from 1960 to 1980 and came from evidence collected from the ocean floor. In 1975 and 1976, I spent four months on board the *Glomar Challenger*, the first research ship designed for drilling into the deep ocean floor in order to retrieve geological samples from it. The theory of plate tectonics asserted that the ocean basins are young geological features, continually being formed along mid-ocean ridges where the lithosphere spreads apart and molten rock from the Earth's mantle erupts onto the ocean floor. Thus, drilling into the Earth should yield only young rock, in geological terms—mainly less than 200 million years old.

We drilled deeply into the northern Mid-Atlantic Ridge at a number of sites located between the Azores and the Equator, removing rock samples and examining them in our shipboard lab. From our samples, we confirmed our hypothesis that the Mid-Atlantic Ridge is an extremely young volcanic field, continually generating new oceanic crust. As a result of seafloor spreading, North America and Africa are slowly drifting apart, widening the Atlantic Ocean at a rate of about two centimeters per year.

Such continental breakups caused by seafloor spreading have left their mark on the diversity and distribution of present-day plant and animal species. Marsupials, the group of mammals that includes kangaroos, wallabies, koalas, and opossums, are a good example. Marsupials give birth to immature young that attach themselves to the mother's nipple, which in most species is surrounded by a pouch. Today marsupials are abundant and diverse only in Australia, but they evolved in North America about 100 million years ago. At that time North America was much closer than it is today to South America, western Antarctica, and Australia. Over time, the early marsupials migrated throughout the adjacent landmasses and evolved into many species.

Shortly after the evolution of marsupials, however, placental mammals also evolved. (The offspring of placental mammals develop fully inside the female's uterus before birth, unlike the young of marsupial mammals.) As placental mammals evolved and spread, they occupied many of the same habitats as marsupials. Where marsupials and placentals came together, as in North America, most of the marsupials became extinct because they could not survive competition with the more intelligent and adaptable placentals. Today only one marsupial family, the opossums, successfully coexists with placental mammals in North America.

In Australia and South America, however, marsupials flourished and diversified. By 65 million years ago, seafloor spreading had created sizable ocean basins that isolated these two continents from other landmasses that harbored placental mammals, including North America. In the two isolated continents of the Southern Hemisphere, marsupials occupied a variety of habitats and diversified into many different forms, some resembling moles, elephants, camels, and even wolves, such as the Tasmanian wolf, which became extinct in historic times.

The most recent chapter in the story of marsupial evolution occurred about three million years ago with the formation of the isthmus of Costa Rica and Panama that connects North and South America. As two oceanic plates converged, the ocean that had separated the two continents narrowed, and volcanoes formed. Over time, the erupted magma piled up, eventually rising above sea level and creating a land bridge between the two continents. Although a relatively small-scale event in terms of plate tectonics, the creation of the land bridge had profound consequences for the evolution of life in the Americas. When landmasses converge, previously isolated populations of species can intermingle. The migration of placental mammals across the land bridge from the north into South America contributed to the extinction of most of the marsupials that evolved there. As species compete for habitat niches, some may lose the battle and become extinct. Exposure to new diseases and new predators also takes its toll.

The formation of the supercontinent Pangaea was perhaps the most dramatic convergent event in terms of impact on the evolution of life. Pangaea (Greek for "all land") formed from the northward movement of Gondwana, a large continent in the Southern Hemisphere, which had assembled millions of years earlier. As Gondwana drifted north, it joined North America, Europe, and Asia, creating a single great landmass that covered two-fifths of the globe. Seaways that had intervened between the continents were destroyed, and mountain ranges rose where once there had been seafloor. (The present Appalachian Mountains are a deeply eroded remnant of that event.) Shortly after the final assembly of Pangaea at the close of the Permian Period 250 million years ago, 80 to 95 percent of marine invertebrate species perished in the largest biological extinction in the fossil record. As yet, there is no consensus as to the cause or causes of this extinction, but the convergence of continents may have played a role.

In general, global biodiversity is richest when the continents are widely dispersed across the globe, as they are today, and poorest when the continents are assembled, as they were in the era

Live diatoms reproduce by simple cell division, but here only their empty silica shells remain, one of many elaborate patterns unique to individual species. Of these living algae about 70,000 species, both fossil and recent, have been described, and that number may only represent the half of it. As small as they are diverse (some 25 million would fit in a teaspoon), diatoms are also abundant and essential. They make up about a quarter of Earth's plant life by weight, and they produce at least a quarter of the oxygen we breathe. In life they provide high-quality nutrition to animals as small as protozoas and as large as baleen whales. In death they pack down on ocean floors, where their oil-rich plasma is eventually buried and transformed into petroleum.

Black volcanic rubble recalls the eruptions
that formed the island of Mauritius nearly
ten million years ago. Now it has been heaped
into piles to expose the fertile soil that
nurtures sugarcane, the island's top export
crop. Where the sweet stalks now sprout,
the flightless dodo bird once roamed, hunted
to extinction within 90 years after the Dutch
settled the uninhabited island in 1598.

Every moment Nature starts on the longest journey,
and every moment she reaches her goal.

—JOHANN WOLFGANG VON GOETHE

of Pangaea. When the Earth's landmass is fragmented and separated by large bodies of water, plants and animals evolve in isolation, which enhances the development of new species. Also, when continents are numerous, the length of coastline increases, providing increased shallow water habitats for bottom-dwelling organisms.

Today there is an interesting, but disturbing, parallel to the ancient tectonic process that brought formerly isolated animal and plant populations into contact. The movement by humans of plants and animals from one continent or island to another can seriously endanger native species. When moved to a new region, whether by intention or accident, alien species are freed from the forces of competition, predation, and disease that kept them in check in their natural environments. The gypsy moth, for example, introduced from Europe for commercial silk production, has wreaked havoc throughout our eastern forests. The zebra mussel, probably a stowaway in the ballast water of ships, has caused widespread economic and environmental damage from Canada to the Gulf of Mexico. And the HIV virus has spread from Africa to all parts of the globe as a result of ease and speed in human travel. What might be done through millions of years of continental drift can now be done in several days or even hours.

The slow dance of the continents does more than isolate or connect animal and plant communities. It can strongly influence global climates. The middle Cretaceous, near the end of the dinosaur era, from about 90 to 120 million years ago, was unusually warm. The Earth's internal energy probably played a major role in this unusual episode in two ways: by increases in the rate of seafloor spreading and in the incidence and magnitude of volcanic eruptions. Increased volcanic activity may have raised the atmospheric levels of the greenhouse gas carbon dioxide, creating a warmer climate.

When the rate of seafloor spreading is high, the oceanic lithosphere is hotter and thicker. As a result, the volume of the ocean basins decreases, sea level rises, and water spills onto the continents. As vast seaways advanced over much of the continents because of the rise in sea level, a shallow sea stretched from the Gulf of Mexico to the Arctic Sea. This was one of the greatest and the last of the marine floodings of the interior of North America. At that time, the continents were still drifting apart after the breakup of Pangaea, and newly formed ocean basins brought equatorial waters northward, warming climates in high latitudes. In general, this period of high sea level and others like it at other times in geological history correlate with episodes of biological diversification among marine invertebrates.

We are unlikely to read in the newspapers about the geological changes that occur over the course of millions of years as a result of the Earth's internal processes. But those processes that cause immediate impacts on life, such as volcanic eruptions, frequently make the headlines. Most volcanoes delineate plate boundaries either at zones where plates move apart or where they come together.

Volcanoes also form in the middle of plates above "hot spots," such as those that lie beneath Iceland, Hawaii, and Yellowstone National Park. Hot spots form above rising hot mantle plumes that partially melt through the thin overlying plate. Repeated eruptions of thick lava from a hot spot in the Pacific Ocean have built the Hawaiian Islands. Cut off from other landmasses, oceanic islands form isolated habitats, which leads to the evolution of endemic species, native species that are found nowhere else in the world.

The isolation of island animal and plant communities, however, makes them particularly susceptible to extinction triggered by alien species introduced to the island by humans. The mongoose—a weasel-like placental carnivore—was imported to Hawaii to rid sugarcane fields of rats, also an alien invader. A daytime hunter, the mongoose rarely encounters the nocturnal rats, but instead preys on native ground-nesting birds, many of which are threatened with extinction.

Large volcanic eruptions can profoundly affect the Earth's atmosphere and climate. When highly explosive volcanoes erupt, they can project a fine mist of particles tens of miles into the Earth's stratosphere. These aerosols, which can remain suspended in the stratosphere for years, form a haze that reflects the sun's radiation back into space. Because less solar radiation reaches the Earth, surface temperatures cool. The 1991 eruption of Mount Pinatubo in the Philippines, for example, ejected three to five cubic kilometers of fragmented magma into the stratosphere, making it the largest eruption of the past century. As a result of the aerosols ejected, 1992 was the coolest year since 1986, interrupting six years of record-breaking high temperatures, possibly the result of the buildup of carbon dioxide, methane, and other greenhouse gases in the atmosphere.

The 1815 eruption of Tambora Volcano on Sumbawa Island in Indonesia had an even greater effect on climate. The volume of the erupted magma was between 30 and 150 cubic kilometers. About 12,000 people died in the eruption on Sumbawa and the surrounding islands, and another 80,000 perished later in the Northern Hemisphere as a consequence of climatic effects. Following the eruption, a gigantic veil of finely broken rock and aerosols spread over both hemispheres, reaching North America and Europe in the late fall of 1815. On average the temperature in 1816 dropped by about 1.1°C (about 2°F). Widespread snowstorms struck Canada and New England between June 6 and 11, 1816, and severe frosts occurred throughout the summer, leading to crop failure and widespread famine. Eruptions of this magnitude will certainly occur again, most likely within the next few hundred years, although when is uncertain.

Volcanoes, however, are not only engines of destruction. Volcanic eruptions are also the ultimate source of most of the gases that make up the Earth's atmosphere. As they erupt beneath the sea and on land, volcanic gases are noxious to life. They are highly acidic and lack free, or uncombined, oxygen, used by organisms for respiration. Yet over geological time, their accumulation and interaction with other parts of the Earth's complex system produced our life-supporting atmosphere. Volcanic gases, for example, are cleansed rather quickly through the synergy between the Earth's lithosphere and atmosphere. Because the acids readily dissolve in water, rain dilutes them. As dilute acid rain falls on rocks, it reacts with minerals in the rocks to produce clays, salts, and other compounds that are neutral or weakly acidic.

The most striking feature of our atmosphere, however, is its uniquely high oxygen content. The atmospheres of the other planets contain traces of free oxygen at best, as did Earth's early atmosphere. How then do we have an atmosphere that contains about 21 percent free oxygen by volume? And what mechanisms sustain this abundance, what keeps plants and animals from using it up? The most important source of free oxygen is photosynthesis, the chemical process that plants and algae use to produce energy. Photosynthetic organisms use energy from the sun to convert carbon dioxide and water into energy-rich sugars. Oxygen is released as a by-product.

But when did photosynthetic organisms appear? The most recent evidence comes from fossils with a variety of shapes and sizes found embedded in 3.5-billion-year-old rocks in western Australia by William Schopf of UCLA. From the diversity of the fossils he found, Schopf concluded that photosynthetic organisms had already undergone considerable evolution. Over time, as these organisms became more abundant, carbon dioxide was depleted and oxygen accumulated, resulting in our atmosphere's present composition.

There is little question that life processes put the bulk of the free oxygen into the atmosphere, and that simple life created the conditions for complex life. At night, when the sun's energy is not available, plants respire, much as animals do. That is, their cells use oxygen to burn the sugars and starches they made during the day. Carbon dioxide is released as a by-product. Plants, however, always produce more oxygen during photosynthesis than they use during respiration.

Decomposers—bacteria and fungi—remove oxygen from the air to metabolize organic material, and they release carbon dioxide as a by-product. Unlike plants, however, decomposers never restore free oxygen to the atmosphere through photosynthesis.

Decomposition would seem to nullify the effects of photosynthesis by removing free oxygen from the atmosphere as fast as photosynthesis can add it. But it doesn't. The reason is that large amounts of organic material are buried in the Earth's crust, trapped by the Earth's internal forces millions of years ago. The remains of plants and animals collected in deep sedimentary basins that plate tectonics created at the margins and interiors of continents and on the ocean floor. Burial removed the carbon-rich material from contact with the oxygen-rich atmosphere, thereby preserving free oxygen for the many organisms, including people, which depend on it. Without these geological reservoirs, our oxygen-rich atmosphere would have been depleted long ago.

Over millions of years, tectonic forces acting on the buried organic material created the coal, oil, and gas that fuel our modern society. But as we burn fossil fuels today, we are undoing what biological processes produced and geological processes preserved. So far, it appears, we have not appreciably affected the atmosphere's oxygen content. Rather, it is by raising the level of carbon dioxide that we are having our greatest effect—an effect that most scientists agree is increasing global temperatures, despite the transitory moderation caused by recent large volcanic eruptions. And surely, as is evident from past changes in global climate, rapid shifts in climate will trigger changes to life on the planet. But the exact nature and the extent of those changes are difficult to predict.

Long-term predictions of change will always be imperfect because of the complexity of the Earth's systems, which function on a global scale. We must be able to understand the synergistic interactions of these systems and be mindful of the likely impacts of our activities. Our challenge is to act prudently in light of the knowledge we have acquired. The noted theologian and paleontologist Pierre Teilhard de Chardin summarized the complex system in which we are embedded: "Each element of the cosmos is positively woven from all others.… It is impossible to cut into this network, to isolate a portion without it becoming frayed and unraveled at its edges."

Interfering with Elemental Cycles

ALAN CUTLER

Carbon makes up only 0.025 percent of the Earth's crust—far less than silicon, iron, or magnesium—but its ability to combine with other elements into a near-infinite variety of complex molecules makes it the key ingredient of the biosphere. As organisms live, breathe, die, and are buried, carbon cycles between the biosphere, atmosphere, and lithosphere. From traces of carbon and the types of minerals and fossils found in rocks billions of years old, it is clear that the biologically driven carbon cycle has been operating from almost the beginning of the Earth's geological history.

Despite its biological importance, most of the Earth's carbon is not found in the bodies of living organisms. More than 99.9 percent is buried in the planet's crust as petroleum, coal, and other hydrocarbons, and vast deposits of so-called carbonate rocks—limestone, dolomite, chalk, and a few others. This fossil carbon is recycled to the surface through the slow geological processes of erosion and plate tectonics, though our society's appetite for fossil fuels has lately sped up the process considerably.

Of the carbon that today circulates through the biosphere via photosynthesis and respiration, human beings are appropriating an increasingly large share. Forests and other natural ecosystems have been converted to cropland, pastureland, cities, and roads, or are harvested for wood to be used as fuel, paper, or building materials. As the human population continues to expand, so does our impact on the global carbon cycle. A 1986 study by Stanford biologists estimated that humans draw more than 30 percent of the net primary productivity from all ecosystems on the Earth's land areas and 2 percent of that from the oceans—an astonishingly large share. When the researchers factored in the reduction of global productivity by results of human activity—pollution, erosion and soil loss, desertification, and urbanization—the impact is even more astounding. As much as 40 percent of the potential productivity of land ecosystems is now appropriated by human beings.

Human beings have profoundly altered the global nitrogen cycle as well as the carbon cycle. Crucial for all life forms, nitrogen is a building block for proteins, chlorophyll, DNA, and other biological molecules. It is by far the most abundant element in the atmosphere, nearly 80 percent of dry air, but very few organisms can convert atmospheric nitrogen into a biologically usable form. Nitrogen molecules consist of two nitrogen atoms linked by an extremely strong chemical bond. Breaking this bond requires either a large jolt of energy (such as from a lightning flash) or special enzymes produced by only a few types of bacteria and algae. The bacteria live in the soil or in the roots of certain plants, especially legumes such as peas and soybeans. For billions of years the biosphere has depended entirely on natural processes to obtain nitrogen in a ready-to-use chemical form.

But an important new variable was added to the equation in the early 20th century—synthetic nitrogen fertilizers. During World War I, German engineers developed an industrial process to make nitrogen available to manufacture explosives. In the decades since, the process has been used to make synthetic fertilizers, whose use has grown exponentially to meet the food demands of the world's growing human population. Synthetic fertilizer is often overapplied, however, and either builds up in the soil or leaks from fields into neighboring ecosystems

During the past century, the use of synthetic fertilizers has combined with the burning of fossil fuels, which releases nitrogen oxides into the air, and increased the amount of available nitrogen on Earth. Estimates suggest that humans have doubled the rate at which nitrogen is fixed, or made

Nature's carbon cycle animates England's white chalk cliffs (top). Tiny sea creatures use carbon dioxide to make their shells, which combine over eons to form the cliffs. Rains and pounding seas dissolve the carbon, which flows back into the water for reuse by new generations of sea creatures. Human industry (right) has sped up the carbon cycle by pumping carbon-based fuels out of the ground, then burning them to operate motors.

available, in ecosystems on dry land. Excess nitrogen ultimately washes into aquatic ecosystems as well. Though nitrogen is largely beneficial to life, there is such a thing as too much. Soils and natural waters overloaded with nitrogen can become too acidic for some species. High levels of nitrates in drinking water can lead to health problems in humans.

Other, less predictable changes may be in the offing, as different species and biological communities respond to the nitrogen bonanza. European heathlands, known for their nitrogen-poor conditions, are reported to be declining in areas now being invaded by nitrogen-greedy grass species. Toxic algal blooms in estuaries and coastal waters have also been linked to excess nitrogen from agricultural runoff.

The vast and complex Earth system, of which the carbon and nitrogen cycles form a part, will ultimately adjust to whatever alterations our species imposes on it. Whether we will be able to adapt to these changes, whatever they are, whenever they come, with a similar degree of equanimity, is another question.

Twisted by time, eastern California's bristlecone pines are the world's oldest living trees.

PART TWO

Time and Complexity

The Earth's biosphere is the result of nearly four billion years of evolution. Not until the 20th century were scientists able to accurately measure the scope of the planet's history. Is our youthful species the crowning achievement of evolution—or an after-thought? How does the evolutionary timescale alter our perception of the nature of change, or of humans as a force of change? What are the sources of and threats to biological complexity? These essays consider change and complexity from a time perspective—from time that is unfathomably long on our planet to time that is running out fast for fragile ecosystems.

Scales of Change

STEPHEN JAY GOULD

Our perception of time profoundly influences our perception of change. A drastic change at one scale may appear trivial at another. How can we evaluate the significance of changes that occurred over timescales beyond our limited human experience? Or of changes we observe today in the context of planetary time?

Thomas Browne, the great 17th-century English physician and philosopher, expressed the comfort that a literal view of biblical time—an Earth less than 6,000 years old, with humans created so near the outset, on the sixth day—could provide to a frail creature with such strong needs to judge his own species as the nub of universal purpose in God's benevolent system: "Time we may comprehend," wrote Browne in one of his celebrated aphorisms; "'tis but five days elder than ourselves."

Among the scientific revolutions that have defined our intellectual history and that, paradoxically, always dethrone various underpinnings of previous beliefs in the cosmic importance of human life, geology's discovery of "deep time" ranks among the most portentous— for if earthly time must be measured in billions of years, and human time in but a fraction of one percent of this cosmic immensity, then Browne's comfort evaporates. How can we view human existence as the goal and purpose, the apotheosis of all that came before, if that "before" encompasses nearly all of time, with our belated appearance reduced to a mere eye blink at the end, the thinnest of gildings upon a vast edifice. No scientist ever matched a great writer and humanist, our own Mark Twain, in forceful expression of this crucial basis for any scientific understanding of time and change. Soon after the completion of the Eiffel Tower in 1889, then the world's tallest human monument, Twain wrote:

> Man has been here 32,000 years. That it took a hundred million years to prepare the world for him is proof that that is what it was done for. I suppose it is. I dunno. If the Eiffel Tower were now representing the world's age, the skin of paint on the pinnacle-knob at its summit would represent man's share of that age; and anybody would perceive that that skin was what the tower was built for. I reckon they would, I dunno.

Twain used Lord Kelvin's estimates, then current, for the age of the Earth and human appearance. We would now revise both figures considerably upward—the Earth's age to 4.6 billion years, the appearance of modern *Homo sapiens* to about 120,000 years—but Twain's point remains undiminished. Human time, compared with Earth

Fossil remains inform us of *Anomalocaris*, a two-foot-long predator swimming on Earth half a billion years ago.

It is not the strongest of the species that survive, nor the most intelligent,
but the one most responsive to change.

CHARLES DARWIN

time, resembles a superficial layer of paint atop a grand building.

Robert Burns, in a romantic couplet that caught the theme of his era (and of our own time) in brisk epitome, wrote:

> Look abroad through nature's range.
> Nature's mighty law is change.

If we grant this claim that change pervades nature, then we must, above all, try to comprehend the phenomenally different modes and meanings of change across the range of nature's highly various scales. The greatest impediment to this quest lies in our human tendency to view our own scale as exclusive and canonical. Such a bias might not have led Dr. Browne and his compatriots far astray, for they equated human time with Earth time. But our modern understanding precludes such emphasis upon the scale of direct human perception—for a mere gilding cannot reveal or explain the lily.

In one of the most famous images in our intellectual history, Francis Bacon argued that our attempts to understand nature face four major obstacles, based on limits of human mentality and culture. Bacon referred to these impediments as "idols," naming them *idola tribus, idola specus, idola fori,* and *idola theatri*—or idols of the tribe, cave, marketplace, and theater.

Of the last three, idols of the cave refer to mental peculiarities of individuals, idols of the marketplace to errors imposed by the use of language, and idols of the theater to fallacies inherent in older systems of philosophy. But Bacon gave pride of place to his most important first category, idols of the tribe, defined as limits *"fundata in ipsa natura humana"*—founded in human nature itself. Interestingly, Bacon

identified the most pernicious idol of the tribe as our inherent tendency to read and interpret the entire universe within the strictures of our limits, scales and perceptions. "It is false," he wrote, "to use human senses as the measure of things," to base all our conclusions "reached either by sensation or by reason, upon analogies to man and not upon analogies to the universe."

The images in the mirror of the human mind, he continued, cannot provide a good measuring rod for external reality—for when we mix our own nature with the true nature of things (*"suam naturam naturae rerum immiscet"*), we can only "distort and corrupt" the world outside ourselves. A brilliant manifesto—but remember that Bacon could not know the full extent of the problem, for he lived in Browne's age and didn't grasp the special distorting power of this idol of the tribe when we extrapolate our meager limits into nature's temporal vastness.

I shall consider only two among time's many scales of change in this essay—human time measured by the decades of our personal lives (with a millennium recognized as the longest useful increment we can imagine for our narratives of human history), and planetary time measured in millions and billions of years (with that same millennium now representing an unmeasurable moment in almost all geological circumstances—its evidence often missing from the record entirely, or compressed onto a single "bedding plane," or lamination within sedimentary strata). In fact, a fuller accounting of all scales could not proceed beyond planetary time, for the 13 to 18 billion years of universal history since the big bang lie in the same ballpark as the 4.6 billion years of our own planet's time. But we could proceed downward from human time into several realms of far greater quickness. In a biological world still close to us, how can we fathom the fullness of the adult mayfly's single day of life?

The early pre-Darwinian evolutionist Robert Chambers, in a brilliant metaphor based on our failure to appreciate scales of time, wrote in 1844 that we fail to recognize such a slow process as evolution because so little change can unfold in the day of our entire lifetime—just as the mayfly would remain oblivious to human growth and aging, and would probably view any vertebrate as immortal and unchanging, based on the range of possible observations during the earthly day of its own totality:

> Suppose that an ephemeron [a mayfly], hovering over a pool for its one April day of life, were capable of observing the fry of the frog in the water below. In its aged afternoon, having seen no change upon them for such a long time, it would be little qualified to conceive that the external branchiae [gills] of these creatures were to decay, and be replaced by internal lungs, that feet were to be developed, the tail erased, and the animal then to become a denizen of the land.

At least I can imagine the mayfly's limitations and dilemmas, but I don't even know how to think about the temporal world of some basic particles that endure for an effectively unmeasurable fraction of a single second. I'm not even confident that time, as we can conceive or express the concept, has any meaning at such a scale.

In any case, following Chambers's insight and metaphor, let me illustrate the power of Bacon's primary idol of the tribe—errors based on trying to understand phenomena of widely different scales by the single measuring rod of familiar human time—with two opposite examples from my own field of evolutionary theory: first, reading too much into genuine change in human time; second, misreading planetary time by applying standards and perceptions of human time.

The paradox of the visibly irrelevant: A staple of textbook discussion and journalistic reports about evolution properly resides in cases of observed and gradualistic evolutionary change within the lifetime of a scientific observer, or a few centuries of human record keeping at most insects that evolve resistance to DDT and other pesticides, plants that adapt to grow on previously poisonous soils of mine tailings, and the famous peppered moths that developed darkened wings when industrial soot removed the lighter lichens and blackened the tree trunks of Britain, thus rendering darker moths, alighting on trees, less visible to predators that hunt by sight. We celebrate such cases as our finest proofs of evolution's reality—as well we should, I suppose, especially given the common legend that evolution, if a genuine process at all, must occur too slowly for documentation by human observers.

But our texts and popular articles almost invariably commit a classic error of scaling when they make the further, almost automatic, claim that such tiny changes must represent a standard rate for evolution, fully capable of changing a small terrestrial ancestor into a gigantic aquatic whale in the full majesty of geological time. In other words, we see such tiny changes as powerful only because their obvious weakness can be accumulated to strength by stacking immense numbers of insignificant increments end to end over planetary time.

In fact, when we recognize the magnitude of difference between human and planetary scales, we must acknowledge an exactly opposite situation and dilemma. These observable changes in human time are far too fast, and far too potent, to represent the ordinary pace of evolution in planetary time. To state the paradox more generally: Any change rapid enough to be measurable, or even perceptible at all, in human time must race like the whirlwind through planetary time, converting a small terrestrial mammal into a whale in a geological moment, not at the Earth's own scale of millions of years.

The leading American evolutionist, George Williams, provides a striking example in his 1992 book, *Natural Selection*. The English sparrow, Williams notes, entered North America in the mid-19th century, quickly spreading over the continent to become one of our most familiar birds. In some regions, these sparrows have evolved sufficiently "that certain linear measures, such as lengths of various bones, have changed by as much as 5% in about a century." Of a change of this magnitude, Williams writes: "At this rate, no birdwatchers will notice in their old age that the bird looks any different from what they remember from childhood. From most people's perspectives, English sparrows are staying much the same."

So here we have a change not even fast enough to rise to the level of visibility in the lifetime of a passionate amateur observer, and therefore known only by quantitative techniques used by scientists. But Williams calculates that this rate of change (an increase of .05 percent per century), if maintained for the short geological increment of a million years, would turn "sparrow-size into ostrich-size bones, and back again, about 54 times" during this geologically rather trivial interval!

Thus, these small changes in human time—generally regarded, when we don't think properly about scaling, as the source of geologically slow change as well—extrapolate to such great effect in instants of planetary time that they cannot represent the processes or material of evolution at the larger scale of life's history. We may therefore summarize the "paradox of the visibly irrelevant": If it's fast enough to be visible at all in human time, it cannot represent the relevant process that produces large-scale evolution in planetary time.

The misinterpretation of punctuated equilibrium: In 1972 Niles Eldredge and I developed a theory of evolution that we called "punctuated equilibrium." We pointed out that the majority of conventional, sexually reproducing animal species originate rapidly in geological time (the punctuation) and then remain stable for long periods, with five to ten million years as the average duration for marine invertebrate species in the fossil record (the equilibrium).

We developed punctuated equilibrium to correct a misperception induced by Bacon's primary idol of the tribe—the limited scope of human perspective and its false application to phenomena of very different times and sizes. The punctuations of our theory represent ordinary events in the formation of new species, properly viewed as glacially slow in human time, but scaling to geological moments in planetary time. The previous error had resided in the false assumption that "glacially slow" in human perception must translate to similar gradualism in the fossil record—thus leading to an expectation that paleontologists should be able to document the origin of new species by discovering slow and continuous transformation in fossils collected through a sequence of strata accumulated during millions of years.

Most new species arise when small populations of the parent species become isolated at the periphery of the parental geographic range and then diverge extensively enough to become distinct from other populations. If a human observer spent an entire career living in such an isolated area, scrupulously trying to document the changes in such an incipient species, he would note little, if anything, during his lifetime— for most species probably require a few thousand years for full separation from their ancestors, and 30 years of a human career span only a fraction of this totality. Thus, our human observer would conclude that the formation of new species, by his measuring rod, proceeded just about as slowly as anything perceptible possibly could. He would be justified in concluding that evolution represented the slowest kind of change that a human being could notice directly.

But when we move to the planetary time scale of paleontology, this glacial slowness becomes a geological instant. Five thousand years—a generous interval for the origin of a species—represents, after all, just one tenth of one percent of five million years, the average duration for a species. So if a species originates in five thousand years and then remains stable for five million years, its origin—although slow as slow can be in human time—will flash by in a planetary moment. In fact, since even the thinnest layers within sedimentary strata usually compress the evidence of more than five thousand years onto a single surface, the origin of most species will be effectively instantaneous by the measuring rod of nature's own historical record.

If we move from these particular evolutionary examples to a general consideration of our usual concept of change in planetary time, we note that the same idol of the tribe—misreading all disparate scales in terms of human time—has been identified as a chief impediment by both classically opposed schools for explaining geological history: the uniformitarians and the catastrophists alike. (Uniformitarians believed that all grand

Eons-long processes of evolutionary change begin in the relatively rapid event of biological reproduction. This color-enhanced scanning electron micrograph of reproducing cells in culture reveals microvilli, minute projections that look like many-fingered fuzz. Microvilli can mean more absorptivity, because they increase the surface area, where a cell meets its environment.

Not all geological changes come gradually. One day just 50,000 years ago, a chunk of iron and nickel three-quarters of a mile wide streaked in from space and plunged into the Earth, creating Meteor Crater in today's Arizona.

changes in geological immensity—from Grand Canyons to Mount Everests—formed gradually by accumulating daily changes of human time bit by bit, as in eroding a few sand grains a day to carve the Grand Canyon in a million years. Catastrophists believed that such grand changes could occur rapidly, but very rarely, by occasional catastrophes of truly global scale.)

An interesting reason underlies this common appeal by adherents to such different theories of planetary change. If we misconstrue planetary time by limiting ourselves only to the changes that we can mark as efficacious in human time, then what do we miss (in a human lifetime) that might actually regulate change in the immensity of geological history? The uniformitarians and catastrophists agree that restriction to human time causes us to ignore the major force of planetary time. But the two schools hold diametrically opposite views about the nature of the crucial missing ingredient!

Charles Lyell (1797-1875)—guru of the uniformitarian view that became canonical in geology but has again been questioned in our own times—claimed in his epochal textbook, *The Principles of Geology,* that we should explain the Earth's history entirely in terms of slowly acting, present processes operating throughout time at their current ranges of intensity. Given the immensity of planetary time, Lyell argued, ordinary causes can do all the work required—with Grand Canyons carved grain by grain, and mountain chains raised over millions of years, either truly inch by inch, or at most by piling up long series of merely local catastrophes (earthquakes and volcanic eruptions).

Why then, Lyell inquired, had previous geologists generally favored the catastrophist alternative of occasional, sudden global paroxysms as the chief agent of history? In a brilliant argument about the influence of scale on our perception of natural processes, Lyell claimed that we have always noted the slow and gradual changes continually at work around us. But we perceive them as so weak and slow that we never allow ourselves to imagine such processes playing any role in constructing the truly grand phenomena (the purple mountains' majesty), or the truly inspiring events (from the origin of life to the origin of human consciousness) that mark the passage of planetary time.

The solution, Lyell and the uniformitarian school argued, lies in recognizing the power of planetary time to accumulate any impotency of human time into any desired degree of grandeur by simple summation. We could not even consider such a uniformitarian view until 18th- and 19th-century geologists discovered deep time in a great scientific revolution that overthrew Dr. Browne's comfort. Lyell expresses the transforming power of deep time in an evocative metaphor about human history:

> How fatal every error as to the quantity of time must prove to the introduction of rational views concerning the state of things in former ages, may be conceived by supposing that the annals of the civil and military transactions of a great nation were perused under the impression that they occurred in a period of one hundred instead of two thousand years. Such a portion of history would immediately assume the air of a romance; the events would seem devoid of credibility, and inconsistent with the present course of human affairs. A crowd of incidents would follow each other in thick succession. Armies and fleets would appear to be assembled only to be destroyed, and cities built merely to fall in ruins. There would be the most violent transitions from foreign or intestine war to

periods of profound peace, and the works effected during the years of disorder or tranquility, would be alike superhuman in magnitude.

The gradualism of Darwin's evolutionary theory flows directly from this uniformitarian reform so forcefully advocated by his intellectual hero and mentor, Charles Lyell. Darwin made the same argument for biological change that Lyell had advanced for geology: We deny evolution because we have not been able to imagine the power of tiny changes, well known to us in historical examples from agriculture and animal husbandry, to render the grand pageant of life's history over deep time. In a famous passage in the *Origin of Species*, Darwin wrote:

> It may be said that natural selection is daily and hourly scrutinising, throughout the world, every variation, even the slightest; rejecting that which is bad, preserving and adding up all that is good: silently and insensibly working, whenever and wherever opportunity offers, at the improvement of each organic being in relation to its organic and inorganic conditions of life. We see nothing of these slow changes in progress, until the hand of time has marked the long lapse of ages.

Catastrophes and invisibility. Georges Cuvier, guru of the catastrophist view, argued that we had failed to understand the major causes of planetary change because another limitation had blinded our sight. Lyell complained that we saw the true causes of deep time but could not appreciate their power because we had not developed the mental skill to imagine their accumulated force over periods beyond our visceral understanding. Cuvier, on the other hand, complained that we could not see geological causes during human time at all.

Suppose, Cuvier argued, that most geological change occurred during rare episodes, short even by standards of human time, of truly global catastrophes—from universal flooding of lands to effusions of all the Earth's volcanoes at once. We would certainly have noted such processes if we had ever witnessed them! For people of a literalist biblical bent, for example, Noah's flood represented the one dimly remembered catastrophic episode during human time on Earth.

But if such catastrophes occur only rarely in human time—say once every 50 million years or so—then we have probably experienced no example during our recent tenure, for the probability of seeing even one event of such rarity during our mere 120,000 years of existence as *Homo sapiens,* and our 10,000 years or so of effective record keeping, must be calculated as effectively nil. But given the depth of time, one global paroxysm every 50 million years provides enough oomph to render the pageant of our planetary past.

Cuvier also developed a metaphor from human experience—opposite to Lyell's, but just as appropriate—to explain why our parochial focus on human time precluded our understanding of the forces that shape planetary time. He wrote in 1812 (my translation from the French):

> When the traveler voyages over fertile plains and tranquil waters that, in their courses, flow by abundant vegetation, and where the land, inhabited by many people, is dotted with flourishing villages and rich cities filled with proud monuments, he is never troubled by the ravages of war or by the oppression of powerful men. He is therefore not tempted to believe that nature undergoes her internal wars, and that the surface of the globe has been overturned by successive revolutions and diverse catastrophes.

How shall we choose between these different versions of Bacon's primary idol of the tribe—Lyell's "pervasive but impotent" versus Cuvier's "effective but invisible"—to explain why our limited perceptions in human time have failed to supply the empirical observations and mental tools needed to understand change on the maximally different scale of planetary time? During most of the 20th century, scientists accepted Lyell's consensus, and uniformitarianism prevailed.

The rebirth of catastrophism has been powerfully spurred since 1980 by the proposal, and virtual proof by accumulating evidence, that at least one recorded event of mass extinction in the history of life—the Cretaceous dying that exterminated dinosaurs, along with some 50 percent of all invertebrate species—was triggered by the impact of an asteroid or comet, surely a global paroxysm by anyone's standards. We should therefore force Lyell and Cuvier to shake hands and make peace. They both identified an important component of change in planetary time. And they both correctly, and forcefully, recognized how our parochial perspectives of human time had precluded any genuine understanding of change on the natural scale of our earthly home.

However, in expostulating on Bacon's idol of the tribe and arguing that human time provides such a poor model for explaining geological scales, I may have fostered the idea that I regard human time as mean, trivial, and irrelevant for any conceivable purpose. I only ask that we recognize the principle of disparate scales, and learn to understand that the appropriate tools for one scale may fail dismally for others.

When, for reasons of history and constraints of human mentality, we have favored one scale—human time—as a unique domain for universal insight, then a focus upon other neglected scales—planetary time for this essay—may be justified. But I do not mean to denigrate the importance of human time in any way. I only wish to identify its appropriate domain of genuine primacy.

If my previous examples illustrate the errors we make by applying themes and limits of human time to issues properly considered in planetary time, we should also consider the opposite situation—for a case that could not be more important to us, in both moral and practical terms—where we have erred in crucial questions about human time because we have often misthought the issues at planetary scales. Consider the set of current problems, sometimes viewed apocalyptically, involving interactions of the Earth and human culture, and often viewed as threats by humanity upon permanent planetary health or existence: the environmental and biodiversity crises, nuclear warfare, the greenhouse effect, the ozone hole, the population bomb. Now I love the majesty of planetary time, but this extended majesty bears little relevance to a large set of immediate issues more appropriately discussed, for both logical and practical reasons, in human time. Consider two major categories: Moral questions and the paradox of the visibly irrelevant.

Moral questions: As a feature of logic, moral content arises as an emergent property of consciousness: One cannot ask a question about anything until one can contemplate alternatives. Nature is amoral—not immoral of course, but simply not imbued with features subject to moral analysis. Nature just is. We may brand such a process as natural selection cruel in human moral terms, because hundreds die so that one may improve the population, but I can't imagine how

Strata of sandstone, laid down 370 million years ago, have been sculpted by erosion into beehive domes in northwestern Australia's Bungle Bungle range. As relentless as the moon's phases, the forces of nature continue to renew the face of the Earth.

amoral nature could be blamed for employing such a mechanism. Moral questions only intrude upon nature with the origin of *Homo sapiens,* and all legitimately moral issues about nature can therefore only be posed in human terms.

The paradox of the visibly irrelevant reconsidered: Many processes perceivable in human time, and deemed slow by our standards, cannot be viewed as causes of similar processes in planetary time because, paradoxically, they run too fast, not because they move too slowly. In another expression of the same theme, many visible processes in human time bear little relevance to planetary time not only because they reach any conceivable completion in a geological moment, but also

because they can do no permanent harm at the Earth's own ample scale. For an insignificant moment of her own existence, they may injure the Earth, but our planet can bandage up and go about her business on her own majestic scale.

Most issues of our environmental crises fall into this category, although we often express them, with inappropriate vanity about the extent of human power, in terms of permanent planetary danger. For example, we develop catastrophic scenarios about a global greenhouse effect unleashed by industrial and automotive carbon dioxide. We often envisage a scenario of permanent earthly harm as a result, leading to a desiccated planetary hothouse without oceans

> *Now, my suspicion is that the universe is not only queerer than we suppose,*
> *but queerer than we can suppose.*
> —J. B. S. HALDANE

or life at all—the transformation of Gaia into Mars, so to speak.

But in fact, a full greenhouse, with entirely melted ice caps, would still yield an Earth with lower average temperatures than several prosperous times of our geological past. In our planetary history of continental drift, both poles have often stood over open oceans, thus leading to a much warmer Earth without ice in high latitudes.

As another example, we often portray nuclear war as a permanent poisoning that would leave the Earth both lifeless and radioactive. But, by the calculation of Luis Alvarez, the great physicist who developed the theory (and who also worked on the Manhattan Project to build the atomic bomb), the asteroid or comet that provoked the Cretaceous extinction hit with ten thousand times the megatonnage of all the current world's nuclear weapons combined.

And the Earth not only survived that catastrophe. Life reorganized in interesting ways and moved mightily forward, although full recovery did require planetary time measured in millions of years. The human lineage achieved its opportunity to evolve only because dinosaurs died in this event, thus finally giving the previously ineffective mammals their grand and fortuitous chance.

For an odd set of disparate reasons—ranging from a deep moral concern, easily confused with spatial and temporal depths of consequences, to our old sins of arrogance and parochialism (Bacon's idol of the tribe once again)—we tend to express our legitimate fears about environment, ecology, and biodiversity in the broadest and most inapplicable terms of planetary time. That is, we proclaim ourselves stewards of the planet (a better metaphor at least than previous assertions about lords of all, but still a form of arrogance), or we fear

that our environmental depredations will permanently harm, if not destroy, the Earth for her geological duration—as in the worst-case scenarios sketched above for greenhouse warming or nuclear destruction.

In one sense, an environmentalist using the rhetoric of permanent apocalypse might say: I admit that such statements about planetary destruction might seem a bit hyperbolic, but what harm have we done by exaggerating a legitimate point in order to focus public attention? Such may be the customary rhetoric of persuasion, but any overblown argument breeds the considerable danger of clever table-turning by your adversaries— as has happened again and again in this arena, hence my own strong feelings about the fallacy of describing genuine dangers of human time in inapplicable terms of planetary time.

In fact, the pro-development lobby presses this theme constantly against environmentalists making the same inappropriate argument based on planetary time. They may say, "Why worry if we lose even a large fraction of the earth's species to anthropogenic extinction? After all, no species is immortal; all become extinct. Moreover, mass extinctions clear ecological space for interesting developments down the evolutionary road."

Only one principled argument can counter this deep fallacy of scaling. Environmentalists must drop their rhetoric about deep time and recognize that the crises they fear are entirely real and truly scary. But these crises unfold in human time, and humans never need to excuse themselves for devoting their passion and concern to issues legitimately within the compass of human time alone. Instead, we must learn to celebrate, vigorously and muscularly, the relatively small span of human time as the only proper domain for moral questions about the natural world, and for almost all practical concerns about anthropogenic change. We need no apology for focusing on human time. We have a perfectly legitimate parochial interest in our own lives, our children, our bloodlines, the glories of our cultures, the integrated beauties of art and environment, and the species that happen to share the planet with us at this particular geological moment.

Yes, a full greenhouse will not injure the Earth in planetary time, but melted ice caps will drown most of our major cities (built at sea level as ports and harbors), and shifting agricultural belts will disrupt our populations. Yes, the megatonnage of a nuclear war may count as a mere blip compared with the force of the late Cretaceous bolide. But an all-out nuclear war will destroy our friends, our lovers, our cultures, and ourselves, perhaps even our entire species (though bacteria and beetles will pull through).

What could be more irrelevant to both our moral and practical concerns than the evolutionary assurance of deep time—that ten million years after a mass extinction unleashed by nuclear holocaust, the Earth's fauna will recover and move on in interesting ways? *Homo sapiens* enjoys virtually no prospect of lasting ten million years, not to mention our family lineage or our local culture.

We have every right to protect what we legitimately admire in ourselves, so long as we do so by reciprocal precepts of the golden rule. The prospect—even the virtually assured fact—of planetary recovery in ten million years can only mark an inappropriate scale for such inquiries. To say that we should allow a species to die by preventable human disruption of habitat, because all species must die in the fullness of geological time, makes about as much sense as refusing to treat an easily curable childhood

infection because each human being must eventually perish.

This plea, to use the appropriate scale of human time for most questions about our relationship with the natural world, raises a final point about human uniqueness—another reason for regarding human time with affection and respect, and not with denigration for its temporal triviality relative to planetary time. During most of planetary history, very few questions of any kind could have been meaningfully posed at the scale I have labeled as human time. Only the evolutionary invention of human consciousness, the most powerful biological innovation (in terms of potential for imposing changes at all scales) since the origin of life itself, has made human time a relevant scale for consideration at all.

In terms of potential for change at unexampled rapidity, human culture and scientific invention represent the most potent force ever unleashed upon our planet. Biological evolution, at its most rapid conceivable rate (faster by far than our previous example of a 54-fold expansion from sparrow-to-ostrich-and-back-again in a million years), cannot possibly achieve even one percent of the potential speed of human cultural change.

Cretaceous bolides may be much more potent for a moment, but such impacts occur too rarely to affect the Earth in a sustained manner. So long as human culture endures, the Earth will face the unprecedented power of a force for change that, in a mere 10,000 years—an effectively unmeasurable moment of planetary time—has transformed the surface of this planet by agriculture, urban design, and the technologies of a thousand inventions, from gunpowder to the mariner's compass, in a manner so rapid and to an extent so unprecedented that the magnitude of difference from previous patterns can only inspire astonishment.

So long, that is, as human culture endures. And this feature of our lives, ultimately, remains up to us. We may never exceed the Cretaceous bolide in potency or immediate effect. But we may also use our mental and moral might to win the greatest evolutionary prize of all: persistence into earthly time. The novel forces that make the small scale of our human moment so relevant for the first time in our planet's history represent both our greatest danger and our finest hope.

A literary epilogue from Charles Lyell provides a memorable image for this immediacy of human might. In *The Principles of Geology*, Lyell wrote at length about Mount Vesuvius, the classical icon of a natural catastrophe in human time. What spot on Earth could better illustrate nature's power over frail humanity? The volcano killed the greatest of Roman naturalists, Pliny the Elder, in A.D. 79 (in the same eruption that buried Pompeii and Herculaneum), when he sailed his ship too close and went ashore in his combined scientific and human desire to make observations and to aid his friends.

(This image of Pliny's death with his boots on remained so evocative that 1,500 years later, another hero of this essay, Francis Bacon, remembered the tale as he lay dying, also as a consequence of a scientific experiment—not nearly as dramatically, but just as finally. Bacon, wishing to learn if cold would retard putrefaction, stopped his carriage on a winter day, bought a hen from a poultry woman, stuffed it with snow, and died several days later from bronchitis brought on by overexposure. In a last letter, he wrote to the friend who sheltered him in his final illness: "I was likely to have had the fortune of Caius Plinius the elder, who lost his life by trying an experiment about the burning of the mountain Vesuvius: for I was also desirous to try an experiment or two... As for the experiment itself, it succeeded excellently well; but ... I was taken ... with this fit of sickness.")

Lyell pointed out that however spectacular Vesuvius had been in eruption, however destructive (or merely efficacious) in shaping local history, even this primary symbol of natural catastrophe could never match the immediate power of human action—even in Roman times, before the invention of gunpowder, not to mention nuclear weaponry.

Vesuvius, Lyell noted, posed its greatest danger in human time, in 73 B.C., when Spartacus housed his revolutionary army of slaves in the then-dormant crater, and not in A.D. 79, when the mountain erupted. Spartacus almost conquered the Roman empire, while Vesuvius could only bury a city or two. But Spartacus survives only as a dim memory today, a mere 2,000 years later, while Vesuvius still looms over Naples, a symbol (and sometimes an actuality) of the continuity that forges planetary history. Lyell wrote:

The inhabitants, indeed, have enjoyed no immunity from the calamities which are the lot of mankind; but the principal evils which they have suffered must be attributed to moral, not to physical causes—to disastrous events over which man might have exercised a control, rather than to the inevitable catastrophes which result from subterranean agency. When Spartacus encamped his army of ten thousand gladiators in the old extinct crater of Vesuvius, the volcano was more justly a subject of terror to the Campania, than it has ever been since the rekindling of its fires.

Time in Rocks, History in Bones

ALAN CUTLER AND ANNA K. BEHRENSMEYER

Our planet has undergone changes almost impossible for our finite brains to imagine. Oceans have come and gone; mountain ranges have risen and eroded to nothing; ice sheets have covered continents and then receded; species and entire ecosystems have evolved, thrived, and perished. Understanding the processes that caused these changes and their continuing consequences for the biosphere is essential for understanding how our planet works. But most of these events occurred long before any human eyes were present to witness them and spanned periods of time too vast for any human mind to comprehend.

How, then, can we know anything about them? And how can we test our ideas? One can't grow mountains or ice caps in the laboratory or conduct repeated experiments on extinct dinosaurs and woolly mammoths. But the rise of computer technology over the second half of the 20th century has made it possible to generate computer models of many large-scale phenomena—mountain ranges, global climate cycles, entire biological populations—that are impossible to study in real time.

Computer models of the general circulation of the Earth's atmosphere and oceans allow climate researchers to experiment with different arrangements of continents and oceans over the globe. They can simulate climate patterns at times in the geological past when the Earth's tectonic plates were configured differently. They can compare the results with climatically informative fossils and geological deposits from that period—warm-water corals, desert dunes, or glacial till—to test and refine the computer models, increasing their value for predicting future climate shifts.

The ultimate source of our information about our planet's eventful past is still the geologic record of fossils and rock strata, though. Paleontologists, for example, have long been troubled by the incomplete and obviously biased sample that fossils provide of ancient life. For any given species, it's usually only those anatomical parts that can resist decay—bones, teeth, shells, and the cuticles of leaves—that survive as fossils. And within any ecosystem, it's usually only those species with tough, resistant skeletons that are preserved in abundance, if at all. Depending on the vagaries of sedimentation and burial of fossils, some types of habitats, some geographic areas, and some intervals of geologic time have rich fossil records, while others are virtually unknown.

In 1940 the Russian paleontologist I. A. Efremov proposed that if these biasing factors were themselves subjected to rigorous study—by systematically comparing decay rates among organisms or comparing burial rates in different habitats—then paleontologists could account for them, sharpening and solidifying their conclusions about the past. Efremov called this new approach taphonomy, literally the "laws of burial." The concept lay almost dormant among American and Western European scientists until the late 1960s and early 1970s, when it was revived by paleontologists using the fossil record to test new ideas of ecological and evolutionary change—particularly those relating to human evolution.

At various sites in East and South Africa, the teeth and bones of early hominids such as *Australopithecus* could be found among the abundantly preserved bones of other species of mammals—elephants, pigs, antelopes, many similar to species living in the African savanna today. But the fossil species and their relative proportions often changed from layer to layer in the deposits. Did

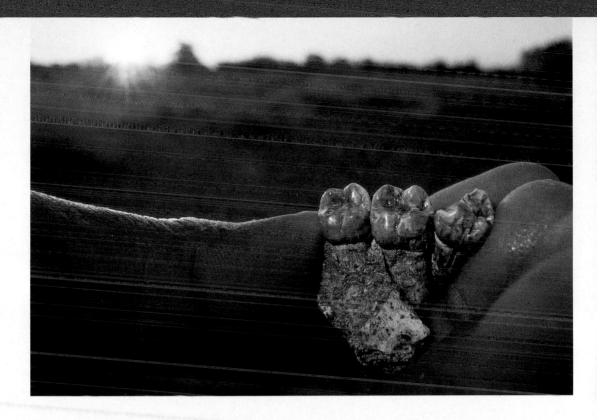

With no written language, humankind's earliest ancestors left only their bones to communicate with their descendants. A four-million-year-old set of fossil hominid teeth, found in East Africa's Lake Turkana region, is an incomplete yet valuable data set for modern humans to study.

these changes represent ecological shifts that might have influenced human evolution? Or were the changes just flukes of preservation? To answer these questions, taphonomic researchers have spent years of field research surveying the bones, sediments, and animal populations of present-day African habitats, such as Kenya's Amboseli Park, to determine how faithfully bones accumulating on a land surface (later to be buried) represent the community of animals living there, and whether the bones themselves might yield information about the conditions of their burial.

The picture emerging from this work has been encouraging. Bone accumulations do indeed provide an informative census of the common species in the kinds of habitats in which our fossil ancestors lived. Biases do exist—the durable bones of large species such as elephants tend to be disproportionately preserved, for example—and those biases are relatively consistent and predictable. The success of this taphonomic research interests wildlife scientists, for whom maintaining accurate census records of certain species is often difficult and expensive. It is far easier to census dead animals than living ones, and the bone accumulations record years to decades of an ecosystem's dynamics rather than single months or seasons.

For students of Earth's past, taphonomy confirms that the fossil record is an invaluable record of past ecological change. Even for habitats and species that are relatively similar to today's, the range of possible variations and their complicated patterns of change extend far beyond what can be found simply by studying modern ecosystems. The ecological past is not directly comparable to the present or the future, but it can give us insight into the sort of change that is possible.

The Pleasures of Change

DORION SAGAN AND ERIC D. SCHNEIDER

Many harsh critics of Darwin's theory of evolution were physicists. The idea that complexity could arise naturally from chaos appeared to defy the newly formulated laws of thermodynamics. Later advances in biology and physics showed thermodynamics and evolution to be not only compatible but intimately connected.

The strange facts that the human mind is able to imagine eternity and that it is perpetually fascinated with numbers, geometric shapes, and other changeless forms have together had a dramatic impact on our perception of reality. For the last few centuries, the timeless has been epitomized by the mathematical equations of the physicist, who has tried, ever since Newton, to discover eternal laws behind our changing natural world. It is curious that we should be so obsessed with the eternal when we live in a world of incessant change, where perhaps the most truly incorruptible, eternal, and changeless thing is our ability to even imagine such permanence!

In ancient Greece, Pythagoras led a cult that worshiped the triangle as a perfect form and believed that numbers have a separate existence outside of time. Numbers, used for proofs, can establish truths unequivocally. An idea, true for all time, will not change (as things influenced by time do) and is therefore eternal.

After Pythagoras came Parmenides, who influenced not only the Greek philosopher-scientists but the entire course of Western thought. Parmenides preached Being, and the logical impossibility of change, arguing that something always was what it was and was not what it was not, and therefore could never become what it was not. He had a greater influence than did his intellectual rival Heracleitus, the poet of Becoming, who held the opposite conviction: that change, not permanence, was the ultimate reality. Parmenides could not deny the evidence for change perceived by the senses; instead he elevated reason, which could intuit the changeless, above the senses, which he considered untrustworthy.

Later, Plato—who named one of his dialogues *Parmenides*—also became enthralled with the notion of incorruptible, unchanging ideas lying beyond our transitory world of aging and death, of rust and dust. To him, ideas formed a higher, heavenlike plane of existence, of which our world of ever changing things is only an imperfect, corruptible copy. Through Aristotle, this Platonic idea of a realm outside of time, perfect and eternal, came to influence the Church, which in turn exerted an indelible influence on the Western intellectual tradition.

Moved ultimately by the sun's energy, the seeds of a dandelion ride atmospheric winds and spread their genetic legacy.

But in a way we are in our own times coming round to Heracleitus's way of thinking. Heracleitus taught the importance of change. He liked to point out that even things that seemed the same were different later in time. "You cannot step into the same river twice," said Heracleitus in his most famous fragment, referring to the particles of water, replaced and different, even though the river may seem the same. And each of us is such an ever changing river: Every five days the stomach grows a new lining; a new liver comes every two months; and the biggest organ, the skin, is itself entirely replaced every six weeks. What we see as constant identity is really an illusion.

Despite the usefulness of viewing changing nature as ruled by unalterable, eternal laws, science is now taking a more realistic view, seeing an evolutionary universe that is permeated with change, in which even the laws of the universe may change. In this universe, the Second Law of Thermodynamics, which describes nature's irreversible processes, has a special significance.

Thermodynamics—from the Greek *therme*, meaning heat, and *dynamis*, meaning power or force—is the study of energy flow and balance in simple and complex physical systems, and it governs many of the important changes we see in living systems as well. In thermodynamics, the First Law states simply that energy is conserved; it may be converted from one form to another—say, electricity to heat—but it will not disappear. The Second Law is more complicated. According to it, even though energy is conserved, it inevitably degrades. In other words, the amount of energy available to do work, unless it is replaced, will always decrease over time, because some fraction of the energy will be lost as diffuse, unusable heat energy. The Second Law also describes the universal tendency for things to become less organized over time. If we look at the world, we find that disorganization—pollution, decay, attrition, death—is inescapable.

A more technical definition of the Second Law is that entropy (a mathematical measure of disorder) tends inevitably to increase in isolated systems. An isolated system is one that is sealed off to the exchange of matter and energy with the outside world; a closed system is sealed off to matter but not energy. The distinction is important because an isolated system, deprived of energy influx, allows scientists to study material and energy transformations on their own without any input from the outside world.

Closed systems, in contrast, may use an external energy source to run complex internal processes. For example, closed systems of microbes sealed in 1967 by the late University of Hawaii biologist Clair Folsome continue to survive decades later because the communities of bacteria inside the closed test tubes can use sunlight to recycle the matter of their bodies and wastes. Earth, with its incoming meteorites and occasional outgoing space probes, is almost but not quite a closed system.

The counterpart of isolated and closed systems is an open system—such as you—that is totally dependent on a flow-through of matter and energy—the food you eat, the water you drink, and the air you must breathe. Such systems—from a gushing stream to a tree sucking water through its roots and then evaporating it on its leaves, from a living cell to a steam engine taking in coal and water and putting out steam, heat, and motive power—are defined less by their constituents than by the way those constituents are organized to handle the energy flowing through them, without which they would cease to exist.

Thermodynamic laws were originally applied to machines. The Second Law was put forth in the 19th century to formalize observations of Victorian engineers, who found that steam engines were inevitably inefficient. No steam engine, regardless of how well designed or well built it was, could ever completely convert the energy in its fuel into useful work. Some was inevitably lost as wasted heat.

At the time, railroad and ship steam engines determined the superiority of industries and navies. Nicolas Leonard Sadi Carnot (1796-1832), a French physicist and the estranged son of a Napoleonic minister of war, was irked that England produced more efficient steam engines than France. Driven by patriotic fervor, he initiated the first studies of thermodynamics, leading to the realization that it was not simply the temperature of the steam-producing boiler that made pistons pump hard and fast, but rather the difference between the temperatures of its boiler and radiator. "The production of heat is not sufficient to give birth to the impelling power," Carnot wrote in his essay "Reflections on the Motive Force of Heat." "It is necessary that there should be cold; without it, the heat would be useless."

Heat must flow from hot to cold, and it is the gradient, the difference of temperatures over a distance, that sets up the conditions for the flow to take place. By making engines with greater gradients, industrialists increased the efficiency of their heat engines. According to the Second Law, gradients inevitably break down or dissolve as things become more randomized over time. A drop of cream in your coffee will spread out, never to return to its original state: There are many more ways for cream molecules to mix with rather than to separate from the coffee molecules. Modern thermodynamics bases its understanding of how

Chemical reactions in a dish show spontaneous patterns and complicated oscillations. Such examples of complexity arising in simple systems—in which external energy maintains internal order—provide an analogy for the rise of life from primordial chemical reactions.

things become more mixed up over time on probability theory: It is far more likely for all differences to degrade into a uniform state of randomized confusion than into one of elegance, organization, or design. A living being or a work of Shakespeare would never be expected on the basis of chance alone. The messiness of your desk and the cooling of your morning coffee are examples of the same thing—the Second Law.

Thermodynamics, as it took shape in the 19th century, presented Victorians with a picture of the future taken from the gritty inner clunkings of imperfect heat-leaking steam engines. Its bleak prospect of universal cooling included an icy Armageddon—a universal end of unrecoverable loss. One book depicted Old Man Death with icicles in his beard, staring out wanly at an ocean frozen in mid-wave. Considering that machines undergo wear and tear, break down,

Multicolored bacteria thrive at the rim of Yellowstone National Park's Grand Prismatic Spring — and billions of less flashy organisms called thermophiles flourish at its hot center, which steams at a sizzling 199°F. Harnessing energy from a source different than that of most other creatures, these life-forms survive because of, not in spite of, such thermal extremes.

and ultimately attain a state of complete disrepair, how is it that for billions of years the sum of life has become more complex?

Surprisingly, the rules of change that apply to nonliving systems are also obeyed by the growth and evolution of living matter. Just as Charles Darwin showed the kinship of humans to other life-forms—startling Victorians with the notion that people were not specially created but evolved gradually from "lower" animals—so today we realize the kinship of biological change with change in nonliving matter.

Living organisms function as open systems that internally organize even as they produce waste and heat and disorganize the greater environment. Ironically, exquisite self-cooling life, by fostering waste, heat, pollution, and chaos inevitably in its wake, accelerates the move toward equilibrium. Death is simply what happens when the living organism, obeying this trajectory of the Second Law, relinquishes its complexity and succumbs to the greater equilibrium. Individual life itself comes to its final state—yet, more often than not, reproduction has occurred. Collectively, life goes on.

In contrast to the sealed experimental boxes in physics labs, life has not reached an end-state of equilibrium. Life takes in liquids, solids, and gases from the outside not only to function but to maintain and reproduce its internal organization. To live on. Biologists have a technical term for such behavior: *autopoiesis,* or self-making, from the Greek roots *auto* for self and *poiein* (as in poetry) for making. As an automobile propels itself, so a living being metabolically makes itself. Living beings are natural purposes, designed by nature. And both evolutionary biology and thermodynamics are charged through and through with a mandate implicit in the Second Law: the mandate to change.

And yet change also moves in a direction of increasing complexity, as in the growth of a maple tree from a spinning seedling, in the succession of organisms that emerge from developing ecosystems, or in the finished production of this glossy book from thought, paper pulp, and human labor.

At first glance, this shouldn't happen. The Second Law mandates that things should be doing the opposite, falling apart instead of evolving into more and more complex things. It turns out that the appearance of complexity and organization, as epitomized by living beings, actually aids randomization, abetting the Second Law and nature's craving for a uniform state. Organized structures can be very efficient at breaking down energy gradients and bringing a system to a balanced, uniform condition. A tornado, for example, is a highly organized natural structure, and its purpose is to reduce the barometric gradient between high- and low-pressure air masses—and the tornado will spontaneously organize to accomplish that purpose. Once the air masses reach their more probabilistic state of calm and equilibrium, the complex whirling tornado has fulfilled its function, and it disappears.

Startlingly, life itself also displays such gradient-reducing traits—fulfilling natural unconscious purposes—that one is led to wonder whether our conscious and unconscious drives and desires also reflect a thermodynamic imperative. As thermodynamicist Jeffrey Wicken says, "I see no way to dodge the Kantian challenge. In Kant's conception, an organism was a 'natural purpose' in which each part and process was jointly cause and effect, ends and means, of the operation of the whole." Just as nature abhors a vacuum, she detests temperature and other differences and will destroy them over time, achieving end states of higher probability and more likely distribution of atomic components.

Our very biological urges to eat, drink, and mate—related to reproduction and growth—have their roots in these inanimate tendencies. It is the temporal nature of thermodynamic processes to have an end in equilibrium, stasis, a point of no further changes in state, which gives all natural systems a direction. And it is in moving toward these endpoints that under certain conditions nature crafts an equilibrium-creating system from available materials. Out of the pressure differences between two conflicting air masses arises the tornado, a complex and cycling storm that elegantly, if violently, equalizes the air pressure. Living beings are complex equalizers of another kind. We thrive on the energy gradient created by the sun, and necessarily excrete liquid, gas, and solid waste while giving off low-grade heat as is our thermodynamic wont; so, too, our technologies run on high-quality fuel that becomes low-quality exhaust and pollution. We owe our complexity and organization to the chaos and lowgrade energy we produce.

The improbability of being you is high. You could never come into being or exist as an isolated system. Something so complex or improbable could never happen without an abundant flow of matter and energy. But you are as organized as you are because you are part of a planetary thermodynamic system—the biosphere—which has been continuously trapping and rerouting the high-quality energy of sunlight and producing the low-quality energy of heat for more than three billion years. The replicative machinery of the DNA molecule does not exist in isolation, but ensures, transgenerationally, that this system lives on.

Living things constantly try to maximize their share of energy: bigger leaves and taller trunks to catch more light; swifter legs and stronger jaws to catch more prey. Even sensory perception and intelligence seem to be an adaptation toward finding and exploiting energy sources. The first organisms with heads, the Ediacaran fauna that came before the more famous Cambrian trilobites and their kin, have been interpreted from fossils to have been languid, happy, and dull sunbathers with photosynthetic inclusions in their cells. When multicellular organisms started feeding on each other, concentrating their sense organs toward one end to help them recognize the primeval equivalent of sushi, murderous life began devouring its own gradient—flesh.

If it could, life would take all the sun's energy and turn it into itself. The changes we see in evolving life reflect nature's equalizing tendency to destroy differences—specifically the difference between the energy-rich sun and the energy-poor space around it. And solar energy captured by one life-form gets passed around as others reach for their share. No species in an ecosystem can hold a monopoly on energy. In fact, the entire biosphere is part of a single system running on and degrading the sun's energy. Life helps spread the sun and would, like the tornado without the differentiated air masses around it, cease to exist in the sun's absence. So why and how do complex things such as tornadoes, puppies, and trees emerge from an equilibrium-craving thermodynamic world that tends toward disrepair?

The answer to this apparent contradiction was first recognized by Nobel Prize–winner Erwin Schrödinger; we call it the Schrödinger Paradox. In a series of lectures at Dublin's Trinity College in 1943, Schrödinger argued that life is not some mysterious stuff with special properties beyond the normal operations of chemistry and physics. In a set of three lectures, later printed as the short classic, *What Is Life?*, Schrödinger combined chemistry and physics to put biology on a different track. He saw two processes in life: order from order—genetics; and order from disorder—thermodynamics. At the center of life, he saw the gene (and its yet-to-be-discovered DNA) producing order from order—progeny, as an almost perfect replicant of the parent. (His prediction that life must be predicated on some chemical substance helped spur the later discovery of the DNA double helix and its replicating chemistry.)

Schrödinger noted that in a thermodynamic world, which tends toward stasis and decay, one would not at first glance expect the highly improbable structures of living beings to evolve. Life is not exempt from the laws of physics and chemistry; its complexity and ability to maintain itself must have a source. He postulated that the kind of organization, order, and complexity we see in living beings must somehow be imported from outside the biosphere. He argued that it was sunlight that provided the crucial input. By feeding on the energy of the sun, living beings are able to become more ordered and can resist the thermodynamic imperative to fall into final disrepair. Order can then emerge from disorder.

Temperature maps of Earth taken from space satellites have confirmed Schrödinger's general view. From a thermodynamic point of view, life's basic activity is to convert short-wavelength (low-entropy) photons of visible and ultraviolet radiation from the sun and reradiate them as longer-wavelength infrared radiation. The living systems of Earth's biosphere thermodynamically turn solar radiation into living matter and heat. In the main, the biosphere is a solar phenomenon. In photosynthesis, the most important chemical reaction to develop in the history of life on Earth, photons from the sun are hijacked, their energy co-opted to run life and power the building of the biochemical stuff we call bodies.

Today virtually all surface life, not just plants, depends on this photosynthetic hijacking of photons. The great majority of beings in our biosphere require direct sunlight, and those that do not—such as bacteria living thousands of meters beneath the surface of Earth inside solid rock, and red medusoid worms in dark ocean-bottom sea gardens where magma and gas effervesce through cracks in Earth's interior—require energetic gradients in order to maintain their own metabolism, reproduce, and evolve. Animals like ourselves either eat photon-degrading plants or the animals that eat them. This feeding off the sun connects all life in intricate networks of energy exchange, sending photons like wayward angels through a maze of earthly tasks, and it is a preeminently thermodynamic process. Far from violating the Second Law, life exemplifies it. The trees of the Amazon rain forest—the heart of the most complex, biodiverse, and organized ecosystems on Earth—process massive quantities of sunlight and radiate the heat back into space. Sucking water through their roots to their leaves, where it evaporates, the sun-loving trees of rain forests lie at the center of a process that generates atmospheric coolness (through cloud cover and carbon cycles) and complexity (reproducing life) locally while creating heat waste farther out. Life is cool, you might say, and life likes it cool.

Consider the temperature of our planet's surface. Situated between Mars and Venus, our

The broad, bold veins of a leaf feed a plant's photosynthesis energy system. Sunlight powers the process, but it is this network of veins, resembling the meandering streets of a suburban housing tract, that deliver life-giving nutrients. This view is a close-up of the mahoe, one of Hawaii's 185-odd endangered plants.

planet is cooler than would be expected, based on other planets. The average temperature on the Earth's surface is about 18°C, though the temperatures of the neighboring two planets, solar luminosity, and distance from the sun would seem to dictate a considerably warmer 36°C.

Carbon dioxide, the famous greenhouse gas, accounts for the majority of the atmospheres of Mars and Venus. On Earth, CO_2 has been systematically sucked from the atmosphere by life, which uses carbon to produce the carbon-hydrogen compounds of organic bodies. The result has been planetary air conditioning—the lowering of the global mean temperature of our biosphere. But even more important to planetary cooling is the evapotranspiration of trees, which produces light-reflecting clouds above Earth and spreads out the heat, reducing the differences between cold space and hot sun. Just as nature abhors a vacuum, she abhors temperature differences and

will find ways to reduce them. Life naturally reduces temperature differences. Evolutionary complexity and thermodynamic degradation are not incomprehensible polar opposites. Evolution is a means of thermodynamic degradation in a universe of time and change.

Early in the 20th century, the Russian geochemist Vladimir Vernadsky studiously avoided the term life, which he considered distracting. He spoke instead of living matter, which forces us to focus on physical and chemical processes rather than any preconceived notion of a special kind of matter. Life is a kind of "green fire," and we are, as he liked to say, children of the sun—part of the Earth-solar system. All life is a solar transformer, connected by Vernadskian space and Darwinian time.

Among living matter's earliest representatives were early photosynthetic cells: purple bacteria.

Area of
undisturbed forest

Area disturbed
by agriculture

For location, see map
of Africa, opposite

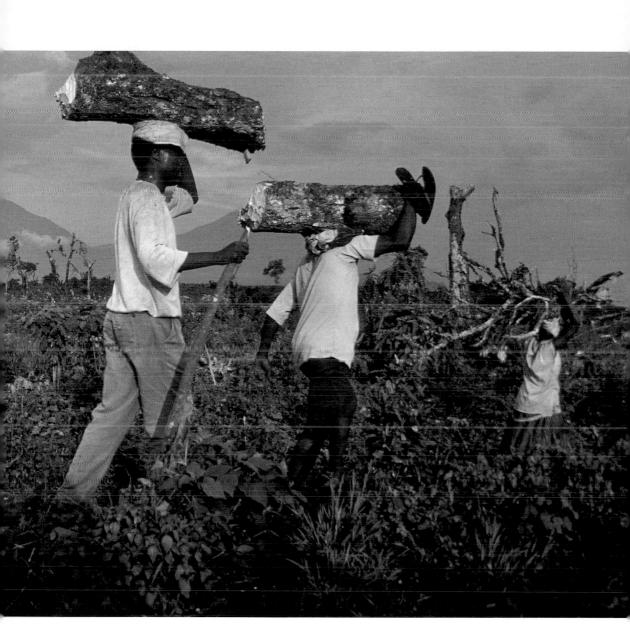

The African continent, birthplace of our species, continues to be the scene of some of the more poignant conflicts between humans and biological diversity. Efforts by conservationists have slowed the slide of the mountain gorilla (opposite, right) toward extinction, but long term preservation of gorillas and other species must take into account the cultural, political, and economic realities of the region.

Refugees from political violence in Rwanda carry firewood cut from the fringes of Virunga National Park in the Democratic Republic of the Congo (above). The park's forest habitats, vulnerable even in times of peace, harbor approximately half of the world's 600 mountain gorillas.

In a radar image (opposite, left), subtle differences in vegetation and surface texture reveal that natural habitats have been altered and fragmented, leaving the Virunga Mountains an isolated ecological island.

AFRICA
Area Enlarged

The dialectic between change and continuity is a painful
but deeply instructive one, in personal life as in the life of a people.

—ADRIENNE RICH

Comparative analyses suggest that these bacteria, like their cousins today, used hydrogen sulfide (H_2S) rather than water (H_2O) to make their organic (carbon-hydrogen) bodies. Hydrogen sulfide, which is spewed from volcanoes, would have been more plentiful on the early, more tectonically active Earth.

But as Earth cooled and tectonic activity subsided, sulfide was less available for these bacteria. Mutations occurred, ones that appear to have allowed some bacteria to alter the chemical reactions of their metabolism so that they could now make their bodies by breaking down the hydrogen bond in water instead. Life had been living in water since its origins 3.5 billion years ago, but the use of water as a new resource led to new waste: oxygen, which caused toxic reactions in the bodies of most then-extant living organisms.

The rock record of rust—vast "red beds" (and unusual earlier deposits called banded iron formations)—demonstrates that significant quantities of oxygen began to build up in our atmosphere about two billion years ago. You cannot read, use your finger muscles to turn the page, or think without the metabolic energy of oxygen gas. Earth's oxygen-rich atmosphere, combined with the hydrogen-rich compounds of life, has energized the entire surface of Earth. In evolutionary retrospect, we can see that our atmosphere, energized by oxygen, is a result of the chemistry of the life-forms that first appeared on Earth. Evolving cells found a way to get at the oxygen in water, transforming the solar gradient into a hydrogen-oxygen gradient.

Later, when volatile and at first universally deadly oxygen was produced, it created yet another crisis and challenge for evolving life. Change was again necessary; in this case a symbiotic alliance took place. The life-forms that could metabolize oxygen were incorporated into the life-forms that could not survive in the new oxygen-rich atmosphere. As often in life, teamwork was a viable response to crisis. Tiny, matrilineally descended inclusions in our cells called mitochondria evolved from ancient oxygen metabolizers. Genetic evidence suggests with near incontrovertible accuracy that these mitochondria—found in the cells of all fungi, plants, and animals—descended from lineages of ancient respiring bacteria who were among the first to thrive in the toxic oxygen environment. Today oxygen-breathing animals such as ourselves not only tolerate the oxidizing atmosphere but depend on it to think and move.

Life's tendency to change and to evolve toward higher levels of complexity reflects its status as an open system; using energy and inevitably producing waste as a result, life changes itself to stay the same metabolically, as well as to reproduce, which is itself an extension of metabolism. But as shown above, life also changes in response to the toxicity of its own growth—which creates incomplete waste that can be broken down by further evolution. The cyan-green bacteria that first mutated to use the hydrogen in water for foodstuff were among the first to be poisoned by the toxic environment they created.

The inevitable production of wastes by open thermodynamic systems means that living matter cannot rest or settle like a slacker but must always be open to new challenges of change. It is to life's advantage to find ways of reducing transient energy and material gradients. Change, both as a response to the surrounding environment and as a necessary adaption to its own entropic wastes, is intrinsic to life and its evolving complexity.

Indeed, the very principle of life is to maintain internal complexity in order to foster external molecular chaos and gradient reduction in accord with the Second Law. Deoxyribonucleic acid helps it to do this. We humans have created pollution crises by our own spread, and by the spread of our technology. But like the bacteria and other life-forms before us, we wreak changes upon the global environment that are the result of our capture and use of energy, and this inevitably creates wastes in accord with the Second Law. Life traps and reroutes the sun's photons—and even uses solar energy to recycle wastes and dead bodies back into structural materials and food. And in doing so, life maintains and increases its earthly complexity over time.

Like an eons-long storm, it recycles the elements it needs into new life-forms and new generations, keeping (in a way that most inanimate matter does not) the past alive in the present. Each of us is a kind of relic, a living fossil harkening back to the early solar system. You may think you are 12 or 30 or 62 years old, but as a material form of entropy-producing memory—that is, life with its continuous 3.5 billion-year-old history—you are approximately one-third the age of the universe.

The challenges and pleasures of life, both personally and cosmically, are not, surprisingly, in achieving some sort of final permanence, stability, or eternity—some steady-state heaven or nirvana of ultimately solved problems—but in the process of dealing with change, of energy flow and all the changing it inevitably entails. The pleasures we find in eating and sex are directly linked to our metabolic maintenance, growth, and reproduction. And through partaking of such

delights, our metabolic maintenance and energy-transforming growth is perpetuated and continued in subsequent generations.

Even those most human motivators—desires for food and shelter, sex and money, marriage and fame—seem to be far-reaching reflections of these cosmic tendencies. Food maintains metabolism; shelters house metabolizing organisms; sex, money, and the rest increase the chances that metabolizing processes will be present in our children, long after our inevitable thermodynamic demise as individuals. In the short run, during our individual lifetimes, we produce entropy by maintaining our identity, which necessarily entails the elimination of liquids, gases, and solids into the environment.

In the long haul we assure entropy production by mating, thereby making new organisms like us that continue the special form of dissipation known as metabolism. From a cosmic vantage point, our interest in life's greatest pleasures—sex, eating, and preserving ourselves and others—are byproducts of the entropy production such activities engender.

We are children of the sun. Our growth and reproduction are manifestations of the Second Law of Thermodynamics, as is the evolution of life. With the origin of life, a kind of rift opened up in the fabric of space-time. The great difference between the eons-long storm of life and a hurricane that reduces the gradient between high and low pressure systems, of course, is that the solar gradient is so immense. Whereas the gravitational difference resolved by a whirlpool lasts seconds, life's creative destruction of the solar gradient has already lasted billions of years.

Life's role, its purpose in the cosmic sense of thermodynamic change, is to reduce gradients. This is what we are doing when we burn fossil fuels, turning oil in Earth's crust into a gas in the atmosphere. Life finds ways to exploit energetic differences and funnels them into its own growth, just as heat in a heated cabin seems singlemindedly to seek pathways to the cool outdoors through the tiniest hole or crack.

Although life exhibits the same kind of manic purpose found in the inanimate behavior of cool-seeking heat, life needs to be trickier, because its gradient-reducing systems, namely the open thermodynamic systems of life, self-destruct if they deplete an energy source too greedily. Thus life, though it obeys nature's drive to bring everything to the peri-nirvana of uniform stasis, is forced to moderate itself in order not to destroy, along with the gradients, the very means of its gradient reduction—which is life itself.

We can trace an understanding of life, its desire, thought, and pleasure. Far from being islands of wisdom unconnected to the mute and unfeeling universe about us, we are energy transformers whose information processing abilities (wisdom, thought, planning) reflect nature's more-than-human, more-than-living thermodynamic cravings—to reduce differences in nature. Our intricacy and the improbability of our existence are offshoots of the improbability of differences that existed prior to us—such as the creation of a universe with its radiating sun.

The intelligence of a tornado is linked to solving the problem of reducing barometric pressure differences. Life, which has been reducing the far greater solar gradient continuously for over three billion years, now has evolved far greater problem-solving abilities. On this view, the goal-setting, responsive tendencies of intelligent life do not look so extraordinary in themselves—they are an ordinary part of an extraordinary universe.

A thermodynamic perspective on evolution teaches us that the only constant is change. Life grows and changes its surroundings. By maintaining its metabolism, life repeats the process of its own origins and its own development, incarnating memory. We become aware of—if not almost hypnotized by—life's accelerating organization as it grows, exporting chaos to its surroundings. Meanwhile, the rest of the universe continues on its merry forgetful way.

We are literally living time capsules; we are museums in motion. By looking carefully at modern cells, we may find glorious exhibitions showing vestiges not only of the metabolisms of the earliest life-forms but of the ways by which life first evolved.

Contrary to the prevailing view of life as a mere speck in space and tick in time, our tininess in the vastness of space is in fact inversely proportional to our potential importance to the universe. We know that an oak grows from an acorn, but we do not know what happens when life originates in a universe. Although localized on the surface of a small planet orbiting a medium-sized star at the outskirts of a typical spiral galaxy, life is a most promising ends and means.

The combined evolution of humans and high technology raises the possibility that in the far future the universe in toto may be grist for life's thermodynamic, gradient-reducing mills. If this is so, then life, despite its minuscule size, may be bound up with the immense task of changing the entire universe. Whether you're religious or not, it is clear that life has really started something.

Microbial Minds

LYNN MARGULIS

For the first 2,000 million years of its 3,500 million years, life on Earth consisted solely of bacteria. Modern *homo sapiens* appeared only about 120,000 years ago. We are the complex descendants of different kinds of bacteria that glided, swam, or floated in primeval waters. Ancient bacteria and their symbiotic progeny, the protists (algae, amoebas, and their kin), invented all the essential miniaturized chemical systems—fermentation, photosynthesis, oxygen respiration, nitrogen fixation, and others—that drive the biosphere. Upright posture, opposable thumbs, and even the oversize brains of human beings are mere evolutionary footnotes to the grand text of microbial symbiosis.

Perhaps the interaction, alliance, and eventual merger of different kinds of microbes even form the basis of the evolution of our oversize, story-telling brain. Animal thought and consciousness originate at the cellular level; awareness and intelligence owe their beginnings to bacterial behavior in ancient microbial communities. Animal cell movement, and ultimately human thought, may have evolved from partnerships between wiry, fast-swimming killer bacteria and their fatter, slower-moving microbial victims. Relatives of both predator and prey are still around today, we hypothesize, in two independent forms: lithe, energetic bacteria called spirochetes and lumbering, sulfur-loving archaebacteria. Two thousand million years later, remnants of this struggle persist. Today the former spirochetes, now cilia, move, swim, grow, and feed only as integral parts of their hosts. Over millions of years a chimera—part spirochete, part archaebacteria—reproduced as a whole new entity and became the ancestral nucleated cells of animals, plants, fungi, and protists. The trapped partners' muted struggles generate movements within cells, including those that propel swimmer protists visible under the microscope.

This evolutionary tale has yet to be proven, but If it is accurate, our nerve and brain cells, like all the others of our bodies, are products of this ancient merger. Thought, then, is underlain by cell movement. Impulses carried by our nerves and processed by our brains originate in the thrashing of captive spirochetes; concepts and signals of thought are the products of physical abilities already present in bacteria.

This is not the way we people like to think of our minds. We accept that computers have precedents, however, in electricity, video screens, electronic circuits, and silica semiconductors. The power of the computer arises from the way in which these parts and others are configured. So, too, humankind has precedents in the organization, recombination, and interaction of our basic parts. Hundreds of biologists, psychologists, philosophers, and others inquiring into the human mind-brain dichotomy have failed even to identify these basic parts, the former microbes, analogues of a computer's working components. Without knowledge of how the original ancestral microbes began their lives and how they have behaved and interacted, we can't understand the mind-brain of any animal.

Nor can human thought, the last refuge of human superiority, be isolated from prior accomplishments in life's evolutionary processes. All our favorite inventions were anticipated by earlier life forms, so why not thought? If bacterial light—glow-in-the-dark bioluminescence—preceded electric lightbulbs by over 2,000 million years, if the protist *Sticholonche* propelled itself with microtubular oars through the Mediterranean long before Roman galleys rowed the same waters, if pillaging ant legions traversed jungle highways, pods of whales migrated from polar to tropical seas, and birds

An angiogram reveals blood vessels in a human brain (above, left), but it yields little information on the business of thinking. Some scientists believe that processes inside bacteria (above, right) may in fact be precursors of our own consciousness.

blackened the skies long before the traffic of cars, submarines, and airplanes, is it farfetched to suggest that bacterial symbionts created biospheric information pathways long before humans evolved? We are not just bacteria, although our cells evolved from them. Our powers of thought and movement transcend the sum of their microbial parts.

Human history spans changes analogous to the leap from bacteria to mind-brain. Our inquisitive and aggressive nature led to our technology. This, in turn, catapulted us far beyond our perceived biological limits. Once, spiral-shaped bacteria had to swim furiously to survive. Now, millions of years later, stripped down, reconditioned, packed as parts of our brains, they still express their ancient biological urges. Their remnants conceive and direct the actions of a highly complex amalgam of former symbionts which we recognize as human.

The vigorous movement, the streaming and flowing inside our cells, is exactly the antidote to death. Life itself is growth, expansion, and nonstop interaction among tiny, strong-willed beings. We cannot think that the microbial mergers and transformations that formed our cells and those of our ancestors will ever cease. Change is the only stable rule. Our descendants will differ from us as much as we do from spirochetes and other bacteria.

What They Will Know

DAVID QUAMMEN

For billions of years, extinction has been a natural force of ecological change. But in recent millennia, waves of species extinctions have correlated suspiciously with migrations of human populations. Humanity's ecological past can shed light on today's extinction crisis— and raise warnings for the Earth's biodiversity.

Biologists and paleontologists of the distant human future—if there are any such scientists then, if there is any such future—will find interesting questions to consider when they look back at the brief stretch of geological time within which we presently sit. The most basic of those questions will be: *What happened?* The answer, so it seems, based on current evidence and trends, will be that the defining event was a mass extinction, a great loss of biological diversity on the same order of magnitude as just five other episodes in the history of life. The rise of *Homo sapiens* as a hunting-and-gathering primate, and then as an agriculturalist, and then as a civilized creature with vast capacities for controlling landscape and resources, will be seen to coincide with this sudden disappearance of other species. It won't be a pretty thing to contemplate. But it will be fascinating to professionals.

Let's posit these future scientists at a remove of, say, two million years. For convenience, let's give them a couple of names—call them, oh, Dr. Zeta and Dr. Glebb. Dr. Glebb is an ecologist who studies rats. He knows everything there is to know about how *Rattus synanthropus*, the sole species

alive in his day, maintains its teeming populations among the old, abandoned, intercontinental subway tunnels, feeding mostly on bacterial scum and leaked sewage. Dr. Zeta is a paleontologist whose specialty is nonhuman primates, an obscure and long vanished group that includes lemurs, lorises, tarsiers, gibbons, orangutans, monkeys, gorillas, and several other extinct lineages. Dr. Zeta has never laid eyes on a monkey or a gorilla—not a live one. She knows them from fossils, stuffed specimens, pickled organs, and DNA files in archaic digital code. The only extant nonhuman primate is the white laboratory chimpanzee, still so crucial to medical research; but the white chimp doesn't interest her, since it's incapable of existence on the outside.

The phrase *on the outside,* by the way, is Zeta's equivalent to the quaint and obsolete formulation from an earlier era: *in the wild.* There is no wild. Trees still exist, a modest catalog of species, but parcels of trackless forest do not. The Amazon is now just a river, a brown waterway flowing among endless urban sprawl, not a region of wilderness. The Congo Basin has been tastefully paved. Drs. Glebb and Zeta don't lament these

Human hands, here stencilled in a south Patagonian cave 7,000 years ago, have altered the course of Earth's nature.

> *To create a little flower is the labour of ages.*
>
> —WILLIAM BLAKE

realities. They are scientists, not nostalgists. They share a fascination with the ecological secrets of survival, and therefore too with survival's converse, extinction.

Having studied the fossil record as well as the scientific literature, Zeta and Glebb know as much as our 20th-century paleontologists do, and more, about mass extinctions. They know that the age of dinosaurs ended abruptly with the Cretaceous. They know that the Ordovician extinction claimed most of the world's marine animal diversity, at a time when land animals didn't yet exist. They know about the Permian extinction, largest of all, and about the Devonian and the Triassic events. They may even know, based on astronomical evidence undiscovered in our era, that all five of those cataclysms derived from a single, recurrent cause—a cyclic pattern of destruction wreaked by falling asteroids or some such.

And they know something else. *Besides the big five,* says Dr. Zeta, *there was that sixth mass extinction, about 65 million years after the Cretaceous. Remember that one, Glebb?*

Glebb says: *Do I remember? How could I forget? The last of the six. The one that doesn't conform to any pattern, the one that's more mystifying in its way than all the others. Falling asteroids had nothing to do with it.* Glebb and Zeta exchange a dour look. They know that the sixth extinction is the anthropogenic one.

They don't know your name or mine, but with the wisdom of hindsight across the long reach of time they know that we, and people like us, were responsible. When Zeta and Glebb ponder its meaning, they ponder us.

Among the less basic questions facing them, there's the matter of etiology. *What caused it?* Dr. Zeta has often wondered. *Humans did, yes, of course, by force of our prepotency, sheer abundance,*

and insatiability—that much is still obvious after two million years—*but, I mean, specifically how and wherefore? What were the mechanisms? What immediate forms of human activity yielded such exterminations?*

Timing and scope are also at issue. *When did it start?* asks Dr. Glebb. *How long did it continue? How many species were ultimately lost?* And they're curious about the aftermath. *How many species survived? Why those in particular? With what abiding effects on the course of life?*

Lastly, as scientists, they need a label. They might know this event as the Holocene extinction, after our own current geological epoch. But the Holocene epoch stretches back just 10,000 years, to the end of the last ice age, not quite far enough to encompass all the relevant data. They might call it the Quaternary extinction, after that wider bracket of geological time embracing both the Holocene and the Pleistocene. It was during the Pleistocene that the crucial changes began— *Homo erectus* of eastern Africa gave rise to *Homo sapiens,* and the savvy primate then dispersed every which way, colonizing all reachable and habitable regions of the planet, with what appear to have been devastating effects upon local faunas and floras. But the term "Quaternary extinction" doesn't quite fit; it's too baggy, since the Quaternary period covers almost two million years, whereas the human-caused obliteration of species seems to trace back, at most, about 50,000 years. So a better label, for its precision, might be the Late Quaternary extinction—or, in its handy short form, the LQE.

Whatever they may call it, and however hard they may study, future biologists and paleontologists are bound to find the whole matter puzzling. Rat ecology could be instructive, but only marginally. Pickled gorillas will be more

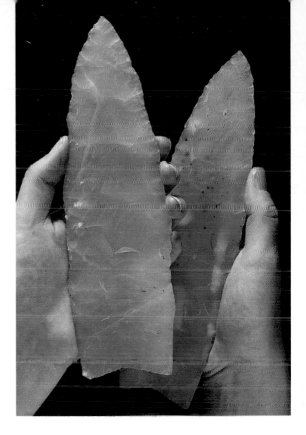

poignant than eloquent. If we ourselves can't comprehend the dynamics of the LQE, or fathom its implications, or account for its seeming inexorability, or prevent it, how will Zeta and Glebb ever figure the thing out?

They'll want to know: *What on Earth were you people thinking?*

In the recent past, the very idea of extinction was unimaginable. Just two centuries ago, well-educated people generally embraced the notion of a Great Chain of Being—that is, an incremental hierarchy of living creatures, each one designed and delivered to Earth by the divine creator. God had made all species, yes? Therefore, who could be so irreverent as to contemplate the unmaking of even a single one? Nobody—or at least, nobody who professed orthodox piety.

The historian Arthur O. Lovejoy, in his classic book *The Great Chain of Being*, traced this notion of nature's divinely appointed fullness and labeled it "the principle of plenitude." That principle, asserting axiomatically that the Great Chain could not suffer losses or gaps without ruination of the whole, had found expression by observers as sharp-minded as Alexander Pope: "From Nature's chain whatever link you strike, Tenth, or ten thousandth, breaks the chain alike." Thomas Jefferson put his own skepticism about extinction into a scholarly paper published in 1799. Discussing a giant sloth-like beast called *Megalonyx* that was known from fossil remains found in today's West Virginia, Jefferson wrote:

> In fine, the bones exist: therefore the animal has existed. The movements of nature are in a never-ending circle. The animal species which has once been put into a train of motion, is probably still moving in that train....If this animal has once

For almost as long as humans have been making tools, they have been changing the face of nature. A set of spear points (top), chiseled from stone 11,000 years ago in Washington State, were probably used to hunt and kill big game like the woolly mammoth (bottom, in a museum re-creation). Many scientists believe the mammoth, like other large animals of the Pleistocene era, was hunted to oblivion in Europe and Asia, then became extinct as human populations spread across North America.

Change comes like a little wind that ruffles the curtains at dawn, and it comes like the stealthy perfume of wildflowers hidden in the grass.

—JOHN STEINBECK

existed, it is probable on this general view of the movements of nature that he still exists.

But no one ever sighted a living *Megalonyx* in the Shenandoahs, and later research suggests that it was extinct by about 11,000 years ago, shortly before the end of the Pleistocene. Eventually it became known in the paleontological literature as *Megalonyx jeffersonii,* though not because the polymathic Virginian had been right in his syllogistic argument for its survival.

Paleontology itself was a branch of science that didn't yet exist. But about the same time that Jefferson published his amateur paper "on the Discovery of Certain Bones of a Quadruped," a more expert biologist in Paris, Georges Cuvier, was doing work that would help others accept extinction as reality. Cuvier, like Jefferson, focused especially on the remains of a gigantic American ground sloth, *Megatherium,* preserved in fossils that had been shipped from Paraguay. He also studied elephant-like beasts that would later be classified as *Mammuthus,* as well as other large, missing mammals whose remains had been lately unearthed. "Many of the animals Cuvier analyzed," according to Donald K. Grayson, historian of paleontology, "we now know to have become extinct near the end of the Pleistocene."

Conventional opinion held that, though eliminated from Europe, these big ground sloths, mammoths, cave bears, woolly rhinos, and other unexpected creatures must have survived in other, less civilized landscapes, thereby preserving the Great Chain intact. Cuvier closed that hopeful loophole, arguing convincingly that they were extinct. Colleagues on this side of the Atlantic followed his lead, so that by 1825 a volume titled *Fauna Americana* could describe ten species of extinct North American animals,

among which were a mastodon, a mammoth, a long-horned bison, a tapir, a moose-antlered deer, and Jefferson's ground sloth. These lost and rediscovered forms were all Pleistocene mammals, part of a very different story from that of the giant Mesozoic reptiles whose fossils had begun coming to light about the same time. The Pleistocene mammals, unlike the dinosaurs, were entangled with human prehistory.

The increasing supply of strange fossil forms, and the careful labors to describe and date them, brought scientists of the early 19th century to a pair of dramatic recognitions. The first was simply that extinction does happen, playing a fundamental role in shaping and reshaping the natural world. The second was that, within the relatively recent past, a major wave of extinctions had struck the large-bodied fauna of North America, South America, Europe, and maybe elsewhere.

These ideas helped liberate the thinking of Charles Darwin, who built extinction into the logical structure of *Origin of Species*:

> The theory of natural selection is grounded on the belief that each new variety, and ultimately each new species, is produced and maintained by having some advantage over those with which it comes into competition; and the consequent extinction of less-favoured forms almost inevitably follows.

Darwin himself, during his voyage on the *Beagle,* had noticed striking disparities between the living and fossilized faunas of South America—disparities reflecting differential extinction and survival. "It is impossible," he wrote in his journal, "to reflect on the state of the American continent without astonishment. Formerly it must have swarmed with great monsters; now we find mere

106 FORCES OF CHANGE

pigmies compared with the antecedent, allied races." If the Creator was directly responsible for every species, as orthodoxy decreed, then even a pious naturalist was forced toward admitting that He just didn't make sloths like He used to. But of course Darwin, by the end of the *Beagle* journey, had already begun groping toward his own explanation for the source of species: competitive struggle, selection, evolution.

Forty years later the same pattern of impoverishment that astonished Darwin was noted by Alfred Russel Wallace, the naturalist whose career most closely converged with Darwin's. Besides codiscovering the theory of natural selection, Wallace studied the geographical patterns of faunal distribution on Earth, and by way of books such as *The Geographical Distribution of Animals* (1876) and *Island Life* (1880) he founded the discipline now called biogeography—that is, the study of which species live where, and why. Discussing the vacancies left by recently extinct mammals, Wallace wrote:

> We live in a zoologically impoverished world, from which all the hugest, and fiercest, and strangest forms have recently disappeared.... Yet it is surely a marvellous fact, and one that has hardly been sufficiently dwelt upon, this sudden dying out of so many large mammalia, not in one place only but over half the land surface of the globe. We cannot but believe that there must have been some physical cause for this great change.

What was the cause? He suspected glaciation. Later scientists have offered other hypotheses. The point is that Wallace, having sorted through data from all over the world, neatly focused the mystery of the Pleistocene megafauna extinctions.

Species of hyena, rhinoceros, antelope, hippopotamus, and elephant had disappeared from Europe, he noted; big felines, horses, camels, and mastodons had vanished from North America; South America too had been abruptly emptied of horses and mastodons, as well as giant ground sloths and giant armadillos. "It is clear that so complete and sudden a change in the higher forms of life," Wallace recognized, "does not represent the normal state of things."

Later research has only expanded the list—and intensified the mystery—of Pleistocene extinctions. North America lost more than 70 percent of its genera of big-bodied mammals, including such creatures as the dire wolf (*Canis dirus*), the giant short-faced bear (*Arctodus simus*), the saber tooth (*Smilodon fatalis*), the American lion (*Panthera leo atrox*), the American cheetah (*Miracinonyx trumani*), the Mexican horse (*Equus conversidens*), the western camel (*Camelops hesternus*), the long-legged llama (*Hemiauchenia macrocephala*), the mountain deer (*Navahoceros fricki*), the shrub ox (*Euceratherium collinum*), the Columbian mammoth (*Mammuthus columbi*), as well as other species of horse, proboscidean, peccary, goat, ox, and bison.

Australia lost about 60 species of big animals, many of which were imposing marsupials such as giant wombats and carnivorous kangaroos, but also non-mammalian megafauna such as a 20-foot-long cousin of the Komodo dragon, a giant horned tortoise, and a 200-pound flightless bird known as *Genyornis newtoni*.

A parallel set of megafauna extinctions occurred on Madagascar, the big island off Africa's eastern coast. Madagascar's turn came later than the end of the Pleistocene, but it reflected a similar trend, with big-bodied mammals disappearing while small-bodied mammals survived; big-bodied

The certainties of one age are the problems of the next.

—R. H. TAWNEY

reptiles and birds also were affected. The losses there included perhaps 16 species of giant lemur, two species of giant tortoise, a pygmy hippo, an aardvark, and several giant flightless birds, including the so-called elephant bird *(Aepyornis maximus),* which stood almost ten feet tall. What caused the disappearance of these peculiar beasts, and of others lost from South America and Europe, all during a relatively short stretch of millennia? Although the mystery seemed notable to Alfred Wallace, he didn't solve it. Neither did Darwin. Experts are still arguing about what happened.

Some believe that climate change accounts for the Pleistocene extinctions. Toward the end of the last glaciation, according to this view, habitats became drier and more constricted, seasonal rhythms shifted, and vegetation shrank away, resulting in crises of dearth and competition among the big herbivore populations and the big predators that depended upon them.

These crises didn't strike every region simultaneously, but the global climatic shift delivered a severe jolt to ecosystems all over the planet—so say the climate hypothesists—and some of those ecosystems eventually suffered major losses of species. It's plausible, it's undramatic, but it therefore bears a certain air of sobriety. Discrepancies in the timing of the losses, from one continent to another, raise doubts about that explanation. If the Australian extinctions occurred 20,000 years ago, or maybe 30,000 or even more, why were the North American extinctions delayed until 13,000 years ago, and the Madagascar extinctions until just 1,000 years ago? The main alternative to the climate hypothesis is the idea that bands of humans, recently arrived on the landscape in each case, hunted the more vulnerable megafauna to extinction.

That's the overkill hypothesis. For more than three decades, its leading proponent has been Paul S. Martin, now an emeritus professor of geosciences at the University of Arizona (and a provocative advocate of introducing elephants to the American West, as a step toward repairing the ecological loss of the mammoths and restarting elephantid evolution on this continent). Back in 1966 Martin published a paper titled "Africa and Pleistocene Overkill" in the journal *Nature.* Since then he has refined the idea, mustered more evidence, encouraged a useful debate, and answered criticisms of his overkill scenario. In *Quaternary Extinctions,* coedited by Martin in 1984 and including his own chapter, "Prehistoric Overkill: The Global Model," Martin wrote: "If man's role in the process was negligible or quite incidental, it would be an amazing coincidence that extinctions of most large mammals occurred when they did." The coincidence he had in mind was between humanity's arrival, in this place or that, and the end of a great age of big beasts.

But when *did* humanity arrive in this place or that? The archaeological evidence suggests—or, at least until a few years ago, it suggested—that humans first reached North America shortly before the Pleistocene megafauna disappeared. Likewise in Australia, although the match there was not quite so precise; likewise in Madagascar. "A rapid rate of change can be anticipated whenever a land mass was first exposed to *Homo sapiens,*" wrote Martin. "The vulnerable species in a fauna first encountering prehistorical people will suddenly vanish from the fossil record."

In the Americas, that correlation seemed especially strong. A culture of big-animal hunters now known as the Clovis people (after the site in Clovis, New Mexico, where their characteristic stone spearheads and other tools were first identified) began spreading across the U.S. about 11,500 years ago; they were presumed to have come via the Bering land bridge from Asia, and to have moved quickly eastward and southward; by 10,500 years ago they had reached southern Patagonia, and around that same time the giant ground sloths and other vulnerable South American mega-fauna went extinct.

More recent evidence and bold new inter-pretations, though, have pushed back the date of first human presence and suggested a pre-Clovis people who might have arrived by sea (from southeast Asia? or from Europe, along the edge of the northern ice?) and who might or might not have preyed on big terrestrial mammals. Mean-while, for Australia the evidence has shifted in the opposite way—from weakly supporting Martin's hypothesis to supporting it more strongly.

The dating of the Australian extinctions had been uncertain, due largely to limitations in the reach of the standard technique, measuring car-bon-14 decay. But a paper published on January 8, 1999, in *Science,* by Gifford H. Miller and his colleagues announced a more precise dating of the extinction of *Genyornis newtoni,* that ostrich-size bird. Improved techniques (including a process called amino acid racemization, especial-ly applicable to eggshells) have allowed Miller's group to show that the big bird came to its end abruptly, everywhere throughout Australia, about 50,000 years ago. This was just after humans had arrived (not tens of millennia afterward, as the previous extinction dates had implied), and during a period when Australia's climate was cooling mildly but not drastically. Miller and his coauthors draw the conclusion: "Simultaneous extinction of *Genyornis* at all sites during an inter-val of modest climate change implies that human impact, not climate, was responsible."

The biggest threat to a species is not necessarily the overambitious human exploiter. After studying the fossil record in Maui's lava tubes in Hawaii, Smithsonian Institution researcher Helen James concluded that landscape modification and predators introduced to the islands by the first Polynesian settlers—pigs, dogs, and rats—have been agents of extinction more deadly than human hunters.

Following a lumber clear-cut in Washington State's Okanogan National Forest, a worker drip-torches the debris in preparation for replanting. But the new forest will be little more than a tree farm, not a fully functioning ecosystem. One hundred years of timbering have left few tracts of old-growth forest land in the Pacific Northwest. The fight to preserve it has involved the federal government in an agonizing mix of social, ecological, and economic problems.

In some parts of the planet, where evidence of Pleistocene extinctions is less pronounced (mainland Asia, for instance), the overkill may have been more gradual and less crucial, merely exacerbating the travails of mammal populations that were already suffering climatic stress. But in other regions, such as South America and Australia, it seems to have been mortally fast. Paul Martin has suggested a speedier variant in those cases—a cycle of human invasion, discovery of abundant and incautious game, bounteously successful hunting, human population growth, onward dispersal, and further slaughter, driving prey species rapidly to the point of extinction. Martin's term for the speedy version is "blitzkrieg."

The most isolated landmasses of the planet, where human arrival occurred late, were most susceptible to blitzkrieg. The most isolated fauna, unprepared for this fearsome new predator—with its stone-point weapons, its spoken language, and its collaborative hunting strategies—would have suffered worst. Madagascar was not just an island but an ancient one, long separated from Africa by a deepwater channel. Australia was an island continent. And the American hemisphere, except when the Bering land bridge rose above water, was essentially a huge, two-continent island. This pattern, as highlighted by Martin, represents our earliest warning of the complicated, fateful relationship between insularity and extinction.

The Late Quaternary extinction's second major phase began about 3,500 years ago in the western Pacific Ocean, when a lineage of humans now known as the Lapita people began moving eastward, colonizing one remote island after another. The forms extinguished during this phase were mostly birds. Many were endemic species or subspecies confined (by their flightlessness, or by their reluctance to fly over water) to a single island.

The Lapita people possessed some advanced technological skills: They made decorative pottery and built good oceangoing canoes. They brought with them pigs, chickens, and dogs, and, inadvertently, a species of rat originally native to Asia, *Rattus exulans*. Having left behind the safer waters of New Guinea and New Britain, where one big island was visible from another, they ventured east across wide sea gaps, reaching Fiji, Tonga, and Samoa by about 3,000 years ago.

Within another millennium, descendants of this lineage had colonized most of Polynesia as far east as the Marquesas, and 500 years later they had gotten north to Hawaii. Still later, about a thousand years ago, another vanguard of pioneers found their way down to New Zealand. Wherever they went, their arrival and settlement was hell on the local avifauna. Evidence of their travels lived after them in various forms: pottery shards, the bones of extinct birds, and populations of *Rattus exulans,* the canoe rat.

No one knows for certain, but it is likely that the early Pacific colonizers killed birds for food and decorative feathers; that their dogs and pigs preyed on ground-nesting birds and eggs; that the rat made itself pestiferous in these previously rodent-free ecosystems; and that human settlement entailed cutting, burning, and setting loose non-native plants—in other words, destroying the existing habitat. Many endemic species of pigeon, dove, parrot, and other land birds proved incapable of surviving the attack. Hawaii alone lost 60 unique birds, among which were 10 or 11 species of goose (mostly flightless), 3 species of flightless ibis, 8 species of flightless rail, 3 species of long-legged owl, an eagle, a hawk, 2 species of crow, and more than a dozen species of honeycreeper.

According to David W. Steadman, who has studied bird bones from archaeological sites on a number of Pacific islands and synthesized data gathered from others, more than 2,000 bird species were wiped out during the Lapitan-initiated wave of colonization and ecological conquest. This was centuries before Captain Cook set eyes on Hawaii or the first Dutch sailor, in a different ocean, clubbed a dodo to death on the island of Mauritius. Ironically, phase two of the LQE was caused by the lineage of invasive humans who would later be thought of as "native peoples."

Some islands of the Pacific escaped settlement during that era. One was Lord Howe Island, a small volcanic outcrop roughly 300 miles off the southeast coast of Australia. Never having been touched by phase two of the LQE, Lord Howe became an exemplar of phase three, beginning in 1788 when the H.M.S. *Supply* stopped on its way back from a mission to Norfolk Island, farther east.

At Lord Howe, the hungry sailors found fish in the bay, tasty turtles, and several different forms of avifauna—a pigeon, a white fowl on stout legs, a dusky bird with a long bill—described by one crewman as fat and easy to kill. The island harbored 15 kinds of land bird, all endemic species or subspecies and instinctually unwary, having adapted to this benign insular ecosystem.

The *Supply* returned several times within a few years, collecting turtles for the Sydney market. Then whaling ships began using Lord Howe as a stopover for food and water. Before long, the endemic pigeon (*Columba vitiensis godmanae*) and the white gallinule (*Porphyrio albus*) were extinct. After settlement in 1834, the red-fronted parakeet (*Cynanoramphus novaezelandiae subflavescens*) was eradicated, since it raided crops. These early extinctions on Lord Howe were just the start.

A mosquito fills its abdomen with blood from a Hawaiian *i-iwi* bird—and in exchange gives its host a lethal dose of avarian malaria. Prior to European expansion, mosquitoes were unheard of in Hawaii. They probably arrived in water casks brought by whaling ships. The disease-carrying stowaways have taken a heavy toll on native birds. During one outbreak, "birds literally dropped out of the sky," says biologist Carter Atkinson.

The important thing is not to stop questioning.

—ALBERT EINSTEIN

One night in 1918 the ship *Makambo* hit a nearby reef. Confusion ensued, lifeboats were launched, a woman drowned, and then the *Makambo* grounded on Lord Howe Island itself. From the wreck, rats got ashore—not *Rattus exulans,* the canoe rat that had wandered in with the Lapitans, but the hardy, acrobatic, aggressive, and vastly adaptable *Rattus rattus,* also known as the black rat, the ship rat, and (for its role in medieval European history) the plague rat. *Rattus rattus* thrived on Lord Howe to the degree that, in 1927, a bounty program yielded 13,771 rat tails. "Rat hunting was an important source of income during the economic depression of the 1930s," according to one account, "but had no effect on rat numbers." By the end of that decade, six more endemic land birds were extinct—a thrush, a warbler, a fantail, a silvereye, an owl, and a starling, all exterminations ascribed to rats.

The Lord Howe story carries three larger lessons. First, human overkill causes extinction, as it has since the Pleistocene. The overkill might be committed for food, or for feathers or fur or oil or blubber or some other organic resource, or to eliminate an annoyance, or for sport, or for no rational reason. Second, invasive species (especially the more opportunistic ones that travel in humanity's shadow) cause extinction. The invaders might be cats, pigs, goats, or other domestic animals gone feral; they might be an especially assertive species of rat, monkey, snake, toad, mussel, or snail; they might be animals or plants. Third, insularity itself is conducive to extinction.

The first two forms of trouble come as direct attack. Insularity is more complicated. The insular ecosystem might be an oceanic island harboring naive birds and ungainly reptiles, or it might be the last fragment of a great mainland forest, surrounded by an ocean of human impact, within which are marooned the survivors of a formerly widespread species. The Asiatic lion (*Panthera leo persica*), in the Gir forest of western India, is now an insularized subspecies, facing jeopardy similar to what once faced the Lord Howe pigeon. Its population is so small and constricted, its gene pool is so diminished, that any combination of concerted attack (such as hunting) and bad luck (such as disease or drought) could obliterate it. The muriqui (*Brachyteles arachnoides*), South America's largest monkey, is another insularized creature, confined now to just a few dozen small forest fragments in northeastern Brazil. The grizzly bear (*Ursus arctos*) of the greater Yellowstone ecosystem is an insular population, also balanced precariously near the threshold of genetic and demographic viability. Because we live today in a world of chopped, tattered, and fragmented landscapes, Lord Howe Island stands as a paradigm for the mainlands. Its three gloomy lessons point like survey lines from the past to the future.

But the Lord Howe case doesn't cover everything. Two other cardinal truths belong with those three. The first is that habitat destruction causes extinction. Clear-cut enough rain forest, and you will exterminate a species of fig wasp. The second is that extinction itself, when it disrupts relationships upon which other species depend, can disrupt communities. Exterminate a species of fig wasp, and you may also lose a species of fig.

Overkill, invaders, insularity, habitat destruction, cascading effects—these are the fatal five. Any one of them may be implicated in a given case, and any combination may interact ruinously. Taken together, they constitute a bare outline of what scientists presently know about

114

FORCES OF CHANGE

the dynamics of extinction. If the literature of conservation biology somehow survives in a dusty archive for two million years, Drs. Zeta and Glebb will know that much, too.

And now it's our turn. Chain saws, the consumer society, government-subsidized clear-cutting to create jobs and plywood and throwaway chopsticks, dryland ranching for beef that isn't wanted, a human population passing 6 billion and likely to hit 10 billion within the next 150 years, suburban sprawl, second homes in the mountains, grilled swordfish, tuna sashimi, runaway cats, transplanted mollusks, mountain bikes and SUVs and Hummers and snowmobiles eating the landscape, poor rural people slashing forest and burning slash to grow rice for starving babies, tribal folk receiving medical help that converts their high-mortality sustainable societies into boom cycles, outlanders using shotguns to kill monkeys to ship bushmeat back to markets that serve other outlanders bearing chain saws: We're doing it all, simultaneously, with unprecedented puissance and speed: committing overkill, destroying habitat, chopping the landscape into islands, transporting alien species into ecosytems where they wreak havoc, and causing extinctions that tip like dominoes to cause other extinctions. Some people choose to think of this modern phenomenon as "the biodiversity crisis," suggesting an isolated event without precedent. I choose to think of it as the fourth phase of the Late Quaternary extinction.

Do I need to recapitulate all the sad dreary facts and dire alarms that you've already heard? Do I need to review all the estimates of tropical deforestation, all the details of climate change and ecological fragmentation and genetic impoverishment, all the extrapolations of how many beetle species and worm species are lost monthly before they've ever been identified, all the projections of human population increase and resource consumption into the next several hundred years, all the trends and hard numbers that have convinced most professional biologists that *Homo sapiens* is indeed perpetrating a mass extinction? No. I don't think it's necessary. You've heard all that before. You've deplored and lamented it as much as the next concerned person. But what you haven't done, I hazard, is contemplate the Late Quaternary extinction in its oneness.

For a sense of the whole, we can add up the parts. Phase four began, let's say, with the demise of the passenger pigeon, a species that had once been the most numerous vertebrate on the North American continent. The last bird was a captive named Martha; she died her peaceful but lonely death in 1914, at the Cincinnati Zoo. Phase three began with the extinction of the dodo, first victim of the age of European empire. The final dodo seen alive (and promptly killed) was on an islet off Mauritius in 1662. Phase two began when the Lapita people, reaching Fiji after a long crossing from Vanuatu, set loose a plague of canoe rats and then walloped a flightless rail into oblivion, roughly 3,000 years back. Phase one began in Australia, 50 millennia ago, when aboriginal hunters proved too deadly for the big bird *Genyornis*. These facts are known. Also known is their sum effect: that in the course of these four phases, we have emptied Earth's landscapes, proficiently and inexorably, to take ever greater shares of everything for ourselves.

What can't be known, at least not by us, is just how far the current phase will proceed. Or where it will end. Or how boring and grim and lonely this planet will seem when it finally does. Someone else, in the far future, will be obliged to know that.

Bigger Storms Brewing

ADAPTED FROM NATIONAL GEOGRAPHIC MAGAZINE

The catastrophe everyone expected but nobody was prepared for struck at daybreak on August 29, 2005, sacking the Gulf Coast of the United States and creating reverberations that shook the nation. Growing from a counterclockwise swirl of wind in the Caribbean, Katrina churned west, rolled over South Florida as a Category One storm, then swelled with a vengeance into a Category Five before making landfall in Louisiana as a Category Four hurricane.

Like most hurricanes, Katrina began as an unremarkable cluster of thunderstorms in the Atlantic Ocean west of Africa. From then on, while growing into the most destructive storm ever to hit the United States, this hurricane had all the advantages. Nurtured at every turn by the ocean and atmosphere, when the storm struck it had grown to an unruly monster more than 200 miles across.

Hurricanes run on heat, and there's plenty in the Atlantic these days. Global warming may increase hurricane intensity in the future, but many scientists believe that the main factor warming the ocean today is a natural climate cycle that has strengthened the currents flowing northward from the tropics. The same cycle also tends to calm the winds that can tear a developing hurricane apart. As a result, the Atlantic spawned twice as many hurricanes from 1995 to 2005 as it had in the decade before.

It was in the years before this increased activity, which may continue for decades to come, that people moved in droves to the desirable coastlines of the South and East. Back then these areas were comparatively quiet and safe, even after hurricane activity began increasing ten years ago. But they're not now.

Until last year, high-altitude winds had steered most of the hurricanes away from the Gulf and East Coasts of the U.S. Then the winds shifted, says meteorologist Stanley Goldenberg of the National Hurricane Center. "In 2004 you had bam, bam, bam. They started hitting," he says—six of them that year. The pounding won't stop anytime soon, says Goldenberg. The change in the Atlantic, he says, "is real, it's not a small signal; we expect it to stay around for a while—it could be 25 years or more—and the implications are tremendous."

Another lucky break for Katrina, but a stroke of misfortune for the huge numbers of people in its path, came when the hurricane entered the Gulf of Mexico. Hurricanes normally have a hard time strengthening in the Gulf, where warm, hurricane-nourishing water forms only a thin layer at the surface, rarely deeper than a hundred feet. When a hurricane churns up the cooler Gulf water, it tends to starve itself of energy. But Katrina barreled in at a time when deep, warm water from the Caribbean extended far northward in the Gulf.

Katrina drew extra energy from a tongue of warm water poking into the Gulf of Mexico. The so-called Loop Current is an ocean stream of water from the Caribbean that circulates clockwise through the Gulf and exits eastward south of Florida, feeding into the Gulf Stream. The Loop Current warms the ocean to depths of 300 feet or more, so a hurricane passing over it can churn up warm water and thus continue to gain in strength. In August 2005 the Loop stretched farther north than usual, right along the path of the slow-moving storm. "Katrina was just sitting for more than 12 hours over the Loop Current," says University of Rhode Island oceanographer Isaac Ginis. "This was one of the key factors," Ginis says, that made Hurricane Katrina "a perfect storm."

New Orleans neighborhoods were deluged in 2005 when city levees caved to high waters after Hurricane Katrina. The city's renowned Metairie Cemetery (above), with tombs built above ground because the terrain is at or below sea level, was still flooded a week after the hurricane. Some residents waited for days to be rescued by pontoon or dinghy (below); others waded through chest-deep water, teeming with bacteria, to find shelter.

A modern traveler meditates on ancient ways of connecting with nature at Scotland's Callanish Standing Stones.

PART THREE

Adapting to Change

Scientists can justifiably claim that as a society we are learning more about the dynamic complexity of nature. The claim can also be made that our scientific and technological advances have increasingly insulated people from nature, leaving them with an idealized and oversimplified conception of it. In urbanized, industrialized societies nature can seem to be an abstraction, something separate from daily life, but all human beings ultimately depend on nature for survival. In these essays, we meet people struggling to maintain a connection with nature as they adapt to the pervasive forces of cultural and technological change.

Learning from Ladakh

*For centuries the people of Ladakh, in the mountains
of northern India, were able to sustain a thriving society
in an extremely harsh environment. Today Ladakhis are
faced with new problems and pressures as the 21st-century
global economy encroaches on their traditional ways of life.*

Even if you know, it is better to ask another.
—LADAKHI SAYING

Scorched by the sun in summer, the Tibetan plateau freezes solid for eight months in winter, as temperatures drop as low as -40°C. This is the fiercest of climates: Winds whip up tornadoes along the empty corridors of desert; rain is so rare that it is easy to forget that it exists. The region of Ladakh spans an area of about 46,000 square miles (approximately the same as the state of Pennsylvania) in the northern Indian states of Jammu and Kashmir. Its small villages are dispersed throughout glacial valleys up to 13,000 feet high. The growing season is short and the climate severe, but for generations, Ladakhis have lived a relatively self-reliant existence, meeting their basic needs through agriculture and animal husbandry and supplementing this through regular trade with Tibet and Kashmir.

A visitor to Ladakh sees a landscape that has been created with great care: fields carved out of the mountainside and layered in immaculate terraces, one above the other; the staple crops of barley and wheat, thick and strong, forming such patterns as an artist might have sown. Around each house, vegetable and fruit trees are protected from goats by a stone wall on which cakes of dung, to be used as fuel for the kitchen stove, lie baking in the sun. On the flat roof, animal fodder—alfalfa and hay, together with leaves of the wild iris—has been stacked in neat bundles for winter. Apricots left to dry on yak-hair blankets and potted marigolds give a blaze of brilliant orange. And as you wander through the fields, or follow the narrow paths that wind between the houses, smiling faces greet you.

Accessible only by foot until recently, remote Ladakh is finally feeling the pressures of the outside world.

121

The smiles and apparent well-being of these mountain people surprised me when I came to Ladakh in 1975 to study their language and folklore. As I wrote later:

> At first I couldn't believe that the Ladakhis could be as happy as they appeared. It took me a long time to accept that the smiles I saw were real. Then, in my second year there, while at a wedding, I sat back and observed the guests enjoying themselves.... Only then did I recognize that I had been walking around with cultural blinders on, convinced that the Ladakhis could not be as happy as they seemed....

Before coming to Ladakh, I had never questioned the necessity of progress. Supermarkets gave us easy access to an amazing variety of goods and products; new roads meant shorter journey times; television was a window into different worlds; and fast food a necessary timesaver. Of course, I knew that as a species, humans were placing a great deal of pressure on the environment. And I realized that people around me were stressed by their jobs, that they worried about money, and often were not particularly happy. I had never thought of these problems as anything other than inevitable side effects of progress. Nor had I wondered if there might be alternatives to development, or considered that these alternatives might be healthier for us all.

Ladakh was still essentially unaffected by the West when I first came there. But dramatic changes came swiftly, providing stark and vivid lessons. Ladakh showed me that progress is, at best, a double-edged sword; that every movement forward, toward a technologically more complex way of life, could also be interpreted as a movement backward, away from a simpler yet richer life. My experiences in Ladakh let me step back from my own culture and observe a very different way of life, one that throws a revealing light on Western culture.

Those of us who live in industrialized societies often assume ignorance, disease, and constant drudgery to be the lot of every pre-industrial society. Conditions in the developing world might at first sight seem to substantiate this assumption. But in Ladakh, I saw something very different. The Ladakhi people exuded a tremendous sense of well-being, vitality, and high spirits. In terms of physique, almost everyone was trim and fit—only rarely underweight and even more rarely obese. Even without obvious muscle, both men and women were extremely strong, and, like many other mountain peoples, they seemed to have almost unlimited stamina. The old were active until the day they died. People did get ill—respiratory infections and digestive disorders were relatively common, along with skin and eye complaints—but the general level of health was high.

The Ladakhis' language, art, architecture, medicine, religion, and music all reflected their Tibetan heritage: Their written language was classical Tibetan; their spoken language, a dialect; and with the Dalai Lama as their spiritual leader, Mahayana Buddhism was the predominant religion. The majority of Ladakhis were deeply rooted in the Buddhist values of compassion, forgiveness, and respect, and the understanding that all beings are important elements of the whole.

Sunyata, or emptiness, a central Buddhist concept, refers to the idea that nothing has a static, separate permanence, that everything is connected and changing, that no one and no thing is fixed. Because of this profound acceptance, Ladakhis seemed totally lacking in what

They fill the restaurants, they choke the streets, but most importantly, the tourists who pour into Ladakh from around the world bring money—and what local people perceive as a higher standard of living. But as Westerners permeate their society, what is to prevent Ladakh from assimilating the very Western characteristics its visitors hope to escape?

Performing for tourists, Tibetan dancers share their cultural heritage—yet the very performance makes the practice less an ancient tradition than a modern show.

In each of us there is a little of all of us.

—GEORG CHRISTOPH LICHTENBERG

Westerners might call pride. For them, there was no permanent, separate self to try to make better, superior, more important than other selves. How, after all, can something that is part of a larger, interdependent whole and continually changing be declared good, better, best, worst? For this reason it was virtually impossible to humiliate a Ladakhi—there was no pride to dent! This did not mean that Ladakhis lacked self-respect, but rather that their sense of security, well-being, and self-respect were so great that they felt no need to prove themselves.

For 2,000 years, the vast majority of Ladakhis were self-supporting farmers, living in small, scattered settlements in the high desert. Natural resources were scarce and hard to obtain, yet Ladakhis had an amazing abundance of time. They worked at a gentle pace and had an amount of leisure unknown to most working people in the West. Remarkably, Ladakhis only worked, really worked, for four months of the year. In the eight winter months, they cooked, fed the animals, and carried water, but work was minimal. Indeed, most of the winter was spent at festivals and parties. Even during the summer, hardly a week passed without a major festival or celebration of one sort or another. The pace of their lives was relaxed and easy. They breathed pure air, got regular and prolonged exercise, and ate whole, unrefined foods.

Decisions affecting their livelihoods and communities were made at a local and household level, with women playing key roles. Much farming work was shared within communities, often in smaller subgroups called *chutso*. Likewise, small groupings of households called *paspuns* helped each other out at times of birth, death, and marriage. These human-scale political structures allowed for flexibility and led to immediate

accountability, as almost all transactions were carried out face to face.

Frugality was fundamental to the Ladakhi sense of prosperity. This had nothing to do with miserliness; rather, it was frugality as intended by its original meaning, fruitfulness: getting more out of a little. Nothing was just discarded. What could not be eaten by people could be eaten by animals; what could not be eaten by animals could be used as fuel or to fertilize the land. When no amount of stitching could sustain a worn-out robe, it was packed with mud into a weak part of an irrigation channel to help prevent leakage. Virtually all the plants, shrubs, and bushes that grew wild, either around the edges of irrigated land or in the mountains—what other people might call weeds—were gathered and used for some purpose. Soil in stables was dug up and used as fertilizer, thus recycling precious animal urine. Dung was collected not only from the stables and pens but also from pastures. Even human night soil was not wasted: Each house had composting latrines. Earth and ash from the kitchen stove were used for chemical decomposition, producing better fertilizer and eliminating smells. Thus conservation and recycling were an integral part of the traditional Ladakhi way of life.

In the 1970s, life in Ladakh was still largely based on its own centuries-old foundations. The region had been protected from both colonialism and development by its lack of resources, inhospitable climate, and inaccessibility. In the old days, change came slowly, allowing for adaptation from within. More recently, however, external forces have descended like an avalanche, causing massive and rapid disruption. Within a few decades, unemployment and air and water pollution have reached alarming levels.

The first motorable road into Ladakh was built in 1962 by the Indian government as a response to military conflicts with Pakistan. But the process of change began in earnest in 1974 when the Indian government opened the area to tourism. At about the same time, concerted efforts were made to develop the district through such methods as importing subsidized food grains and processed foods, building ever more roads, and promoting pesticides and other chemical improvements for agriculture. As everywhere else in the world, development in Ladakh meant subverting the local in favor of the global economy.

This made the region ever more dependent on systems controlled by faraway, unknown forces. In the traditional culture, basic needs were met without money. The Ladakhis grew barley at 12,000 feet, managed yaks and other animals at higher elevations, and built houses with their own hands from materials in their immediate surroundings. The only thing they needed from outside the region was salt, for which they traded. People knew they had to depend on the community, and so they took care of one another. But in the new economic system, the distance between people has increased. The fabric of local interdependence is disintegrating, and so too are the traditional levels of tolerance and cooperation.

The modern economy defies common sense. In Leh, the capital, people no longer build with traditional mud bricks, turning to cheaper imported cement. It seems incomprehensible that building with local mud has become prohibitively expensive, but as land, labor, and resources have become increasingly commodified, people are compelled to pay for the mud they use, for the labor to extract it, and for the truck to haul the mud bricks back to their property. Building with mud is slower; time in the modern sector has come to mean money.

It seems improbable that heavy, processed material, transported over the Himalaya, competes with mud, free and abundant, there for the taking—yet that is exactly the case. Hidden subsidies to roads, fuel, and industrial processing render small-scale local economies inefficient. Even local agriculture is being undermined by subsidies for imported grain, which make it cheaper to buy a pound of wheat flour from the Punjab, four days away by truck, than from the nearest village. It has become uneconomical to grow your own food—an unimaginable concept within the traditional economy. In this way, Western-style development operates to undermine local systems.

It has been especially alarming to see how mutual aid is being slowly replaced by dependence on faraway forces. In the traditional village, repairing irrigation canals was a task shared by the whole community. As soon as a channel developed a leak, groups of people would start working away with shovels, patching it up. For centuries people worked as equals and friends, helping one another by turn. Now people see such tasks as the government's responsibility and will let a channel go on leaking until the job is done for them.

Modernization has also brought with it intense psychological pressures. To Ladakhis, the consumer culture that is portrayed in the media appears far more successful than it is in fact. Western and Indian films and television helped create this distorted image: For young Ladakhis, the rich, beautiful, and brave seem to lead lives filled with excitement and glamour. By contrast, their own lives come to seem primitive, silly, and inefficient. Not so apparent are the negative aspects of peoples' lives in the West—the environmental decay, crime, poverty, inflation, and unemployment, along with the stress and fears of growing old alone, of isolation.

Another cost of progress is the impact on gender roles. Traditionally, the way a woman looked was important, but her capabilities, including tolerance and social skills, were much more appreciated. I have seen the strong, outgoing women of Ladakh replaced by a new generation, unsure of themselves and extremely concerned with appearances. And despite their new dominant role in the economy and politics, men also clearly suffer as a result of the breakdown of the family and community ties. They are deprived of contact with children; when they are young, the rule of machismo may interfere with displays of affection. In later life, as fathers, their work keeps them away from home.

Even more painful changes are the growing ethnic and religious rivalries that I have witnessed as a consequence of unemployment and psychological insecurity. In Ladakh, as in many other parts of the world, development has caused artificial scarcity of jobs and other resources, which leads to greater competition and puts pressure on people to conform to a standard model of success that they simply cannot emulate. To strive for such an ideal is to reject one's own culture and roots—in effect to deny one's own identity. The resulting alienation gives rise to resentment and anger, and almost certainly lies behind growing violence and fundamentalism around the world.

Earlier there had been cases of friction between individuals, but for 500 years Buddhists and Muslims had lived side by side without any group conflict. The first signs of tension appeared in 1986, when I heard Ladakhi friends starting to define people according to whether they were Muslim or Buddhist. In the summer of 1989, fighting broke out between the two groups.

The story of Ladakh—the relative success and viability of its traditional culture, as well as the social and environmental changes wrought by development—can play a valuable role in highlighting some of the foundations necessary for a sustainable future for us all. Ladakh demonstrates the importance of a more localized place-based economy. When you are dependent on the earth under your feet and the community around you for your survival, you experience interdependence as a fact of daily life.

In fact, with the exception of religious training in monasteries, traditional Ladakhi culture had no separate process called "education." Learning in Ladakh was primarily the product of an intimate relationship between the community and its environment. Children gained knowledge from grandparents, family, and friends.

For generation after generation, Ladakhis grew up learning how to provide themselves with clothing and shelter. While sowing, they would discover that one side of the village was a little warmer, the other side a little colder; they learned to recognize even the tiniest wild plant and how to use it, and how to pick out a particular animal on a faraway mountain slope.

Education was location-specific and nurtured an intimate relationship with the living world. It gave children an intuitive awareness that allowed them, as they grew older, to use resources in an effective and sustainable way. They learned about connections, process, and change, about the intricate web of fluctuating relationships in the natural world around them.

In the industrialized world, we tend to live our lives at one remove from reality, relying on mediated information, images, and concepts, Tashi Rabgyas, a Ladakhi scholar, told me after spending a few months in England, "It's amazing how indirect everything is here. They write about the beauty of nature, they talk about it, there are potted plants and plastic plants, pictures of trees on the wall, and television programs about nature. But they don't ever seem to have contact with the real thing."

Of course, many people in the industrialized world have some contact with nature, but it is usually as recreation, not as a central part of their lives. Therefore we have come to see nature as a luxury to be consumed if and when our schedules allow, as opposed to a foundation for all life that requires nurturing, care, and respect.

I have learned by being in Ladakh that human beings can live in harmony with one another and with nature, and that social and environmental breakdown are not inevitable, but largely the result of what we commonly refer to as development or progress.

Twenty-five years of grassroots experience has also put me in touch with the movements around the world that are redefining development and progress. In every sphere of life, from psychology to physics, from farming to the family kitchen, there is a growing awareness of the interconnectedness of all life. More and more people are committed to ecological and spiritual values and to living on a human scale. The numbers are growing and the desire for change is spreading. These trends are often labeled new, but the story of Ladakh shows that, in an important sense, they are very old. They are, in fact, a rediscovery of values that have existed for thousands of years—values that recognize our place in the natural order, our indissoluble connection to one another and to the Earth.

A crop-laden woman crosses the threshold of her house, made of hand-laid stone and rough-hewn logs in Sumdah, an isolated village in the Ladakh region of India. The elements of the Earth are barely altered to accommodate her lifestyle, evidence of her people's perpetual intimacy with their environment.

Along Magadi Road, Kenya

BERNICE WUETHRICH

A Masai proverb says: "God gave us cattle and grass. Without grass there are no cattle, and without cattle there are no Masai." The proverb speaks to the vital place cattle hold in Masai livelihood and in the culture of these people, living in East Africa's Great Rift Valley outside of Nairobi, Kenya.

It also alludes to the Masai connection to wildlife. Over the last several millennia, East Africa's grasslands have evolved as a result of the interaction of people and their livestock, wildlife, and all the elements of nature. Masai herding practices complement the life cycles and grazing patterns of wildebeest and gazelle. Masai herders benefit from the elephant, as it tramples through forest and opens up new pasture. Conservation values are embodied in their lifestyle.

"Masai preserved the wildlife by simply not killing. Their whole ideology shuns eating wild game," says Naomi Kipury, an anthropologist who grew up herding cattle, sheep, and goats with her Masai family. "If nature is not complete, no life is complete," explains Ole Dapash, who works tirelessly for his people. How can these values remain when the human population in parts of East Africa's savanna is growing at three to seven percent a year, when tourism degrades the ecosystem, and when most conservationists advocate separating people and wildlife?

In the 1930s, when Western conservationists first crusaded for a national park in Tanzania's Serengeti grasslands, they argued that "only by placing man and animals in two permanently separate compartments" could nature be preserved. This view, then articulated by British conservationist Major R. W. G. Hingston, remains yet entrenched. Its implicit dismissal of Masai environmental ethics has shaped conservation policies as well as scientific research. Most ecosystem studies, for example, exclude people from the environment—yet local people have been a dynamic force of change in the East African landscape for thousands of years.

Cash is scarce; food can be too. But Masai are struggling to be included as equal partners in determining the policies that affect their lives. Ole Kamuaro, a community consultant in Nairobi, says that this means they must have access to the tools and information held precious by many scientists and government officials. To this end, Kamuaro advocates grassroots collaboration with scientists who are developing a cutting-edge computer model for ecosystem management. The model is unique precisely because it includes human activity in its complex rendering of the world.

Masai are working with ecologists at Nairobi's International Livestock Research Institute to make the model true to life, gathering data on Masai household nutrition and economic status; on the location of roads, water wells, and homesteads; and on the size and health of cattle herds. This data will be integrated with data on plants, wildlife, soil, and rainfall. The model will be used to predict how different policies would affect people, land, and wildlife. It will help evaluate controversial land-use policies—rather than leaving them to the capricious powers of money and politics.

It is highly unusual for Masai to be included in such a project, and their participation is challenged. "Some argue that Masai don't need such a complex tool, they've been managing their ecosystems successfully for years without any form of scientific intervention," says Ole Kamuaro. "I argue that our needs, aspirations, and world view have changed over the years." And such changes

Until recently, most European-based efforts to conserve Kenyan wildlife excluded the people with the most to gain or lose: the native Masai people. New programs seek to utilize centuries of practical wisdom gained from the Masai's long coexistence with nature.

are in fact evident in Tanzania's Ngorongoro Conservation Area, home to one of the largest concentrations of wildlife left on Earth—and to some 4,500 Masai households.

In one scenario, the ecological model was programmed to evaluate the impact of increased family farming in Ngorongoro. Many conservationists strongly oppose all agriculture there, fearing it will harm wildlife. However, most Masai want and need to farm, to supplement their diet and meager household income. The model set human population growth in the area at its current growth rate, 3 percent a year, which yielded a total of 7,010 Masai households in 15 years. Each new household was allowed to cultivate a small plot of land. The impact on wildlife was minimal, as agriculture still occupied only a fraction of the total available land. However, the impact on the Masai was great. Increased food security from farming meant the Masai could keep more of their cattle, rather than being forced to sell livestock to generate cash to buy food—an economic spiral down.

No longer is Masai ecosystem management mainly a matter of applying knowledge of livestock and wildlife acquired over generations. Choices are dictated by the world around them, and just as the Masai helped shape the vast savanna, they want to shape the world of today and tomorrow.

Descending into the Great Rift Valley, a visitor can see sisal trees growing absolutely erect along the roadside. Nestled in a dip of land is an *enkang*, a circular cluster of Masai houses that blends in with the texture of the hills. A radio blares music on the country's state-sponsored station. This is real-life Africa, and there is no such thing as an Africa without change.

Changing Places in Africa

EDWARD S. AYENSU

The cultural heritage of Africa is older than that of any other continent, and many of its people still observe time-honored ways of life. But there is also a strong tradition of receptiveness to new ideas. Can the new technologies of the information age harness the Africans' inventive spirit while also preserving traditional lifestyles?

A few years ago I observed an old woman at one of the stalls of an African open-air market, the traditional merchandising center of my home capital city, Accra, Ghana. A fish seller, outgoing, confident, and experienced in her work, she attracted a good crowd. All at once she produced a tiny cellular telephone, flipped it open, and punched in a number. Business was brisk that day, and she urged her wholesaler to quickly send more seafood from the Tema fishing harbor, some 20 miles to the east.

Today, cell and wireless phones are in evidence everywhere in Africa. People in the rural areas are able to ring up their urban families and friends. Africans have already begun to seize the day and, like the Accra fish vendor, the so-called ordinary people clearly possess a goodly share of humanity's innate inventiveness. But in the century to come Africans will need to make the same quantum leap that others around the globe have made before them. Can they adapt their present rural setting directly into the computer-based information society of the 21st century? Can they bring something new to the global technological culture? Today's cutting-edge technologies will succeed only insofar as they support historical cultural institutions.

For most of the 20th century, technological proficiency was assumed to be a European, not African, trait. Elegant ivory harpoon points and bone blades unearthed in southern France and northern Spain and dated to 30,000 B.C. were the earliest known artifacts to clearly embody the human creative "spark." Had scientists discovered in the European soil the true dawn time of humanity? Then, in the early 1990s, searchers in East Africa unearthed bone and ivory tools almost identical to those found earlier in Europe. Their age: 90,000 years. Thus science gained further evidence that the precious and prehistoric gifts of intellect that identify us as humans first appeared in sub-Saharan Africa, the true biological motherland.

How ironic, then, that sub-Saharan Africa, probable birthplace and cradle of our creative genius, has become the global epicenter of human poverty and privation. Outbreaks of cholera, typhoid, AIDS, and a host of other killers haunt the region's malnourished millions. Africa needs a new deal, but not a handout which, in the past, has spoiled Africans for the hard work ahead. Foreign

Drawing on their long tradition of adaptation, Africans are ready to seize their role in the information age.

aid improperly administered has corrupted many a leader and ruined millions of young people.

Despite our many problems, I am optimistic. Throughout history, ever since the days of prehistoric toolmakers, Africans have adapted new technologies to their needs. This is our past and it can also be our future.

Most people, when they first visit Africa, see our rural and urban societies as underdeveloped. Yet our visitors from abroad soon begin to sense a collective vitality and restless energy that have waited too long for proper employment. I have watched this phenomena all my life and have concluded that African societies in all their diversity may actually be highly advanced settings for training in computer science and technology. Think of how Japan's cultural tradition of miniaturization fed directly into their amazing success in consumer electronics. In this new century, who knows what valuable cultural nuggets—ways of thinking, working, and looking at the world—will be found among the many peoples of Africa?

Many of our illustrious epochs—the Queen of Sheba's Ethiopian Line of Kings, Great Zimbabwe with its magnificent stonework, and the peaceful and prosperous reign of the knights of Zinder in the Sahel, for example—are probably unfamiliar to most non-African readers, and even to many Africans. The achievements of precolonial African civilizations were ignored or denied by European scholars until just the last few decades. They refused to believe that Africans had a cultural heritage of such sophistication. But precolonial Africans had made technological advances in fields ranging from metalworking to medicine.

Iron smelting first appeared in sub-Saharan Africa in the first millennium B.C. Whether this technology came by diffusion from cultures elsewhere or was independently invented by black Africans is a point of scholarly controversy. But it is clear that Africans developed a variety of unique smelting techniques, leaving no doubt as to their ingenuity and keen inventive spirit. The village furnaces designed by African ironsmiths forged steel at high temperatures not obtainable in European blast furnaces until 2,000 years later. It was perhaps from these dispersed furnaces of Iron Age Africa that the sword was first "drawn from the stone," as the magic of the early makers of steel blades was described in the legends of King Arthur.

Africans employed their skills with the blade to save human lives, too. Sophisticated surgical practices such as cesarean sections and the suturing of blood vessels and intestines were known to African healers centuries ago. There are records of Masai surgeons performing operations to remove abcesses of the liver and spleen. Inflamed tonsils were treated by scarification. As more information has become available about ancient African civilization, the more impressive their technological, medical, and mathematical achievements have become.

If ancient Africa was such fertile ground for technological innovation, why is it now lagging behind the rest of the world? While the story is long and complicated, we can view a few selected snapshots from the seasons of Africa's colonial discontent by way of explanation.

From the earliest days of Arab and Islamic slavers to latter-day seekers of mineral wealth, various foreign elements increasingly determined the region's economic fate. With quick profits to gain and inflexible quotas to meet, the foreigners discounted Africa's best talent and somehow suppressed Africa's genuine inventive genius. At best, the outsiders viewed the indigenous peoples as

African physicians (above) perform delicate open-heart surgery in an Ivory Coast
hospital. Doctors formerly had to be educated overseas, but now African medical schools
are increasingly able to provide the necessary training. Drawing on older traditions,
a Ghanaian herbalist (below) offers his customers cures for a wide variety of ailments.

curiosities—living ethnological specimens rather than fellow human beings. Thus was the stage set for disaster.

Tragedy touched Africans through economic adventures administered by outsiders, themselves the servants of distant potentates. Beginning in the early 1500s, the Portuguese established in Africa a plantation system of monoculture based on slavery, later exported to the New World by European opportunists. This shameful trade in human beings endured for centuries.

The colonial era in Africa truly took its grim shape in the late 1800s, as the various European powers vied for pieces of the continent's wealth. On November 15, 1884, Otto von Bismarck hosted a gathering of his squabbling European associates in Berlin to divvy up in a gentlemanly fashion the spoils of the colonial land grab. They cared nothing for the self-determination of the Africans, of course; they drew boundaries for no other reason than to suit their own colonial economic and political ambitions. What they drafted were lines of infamy in an arbitrary grid work across the map of Africa. Today bad old borders separate friends, crowd enemies together, and generate mischief everywhere. And the hell it would entail at this late date to fix these poorly conceived national boundaries is too painful to contemplate.

In 1890 Leopold of Belgium launched his commercial invasion of the Congo to bring out rubber. And so the cultural and economic rape, as some scholars see it, began in earnest. To add yet another insult, cattle imported from India at about the same time brought the great plague of rinderpest. This insidious disease wiped out as much as 90 percent of African domestic cattle, with catastrophic impacts on many indigenous African societies.

Yet even ill winds blow some good. Africans have in some ways benefited from their one-sided partnerships with European empires. There are some English-speaking West Africans who, in view of recent homegrown dictatorships, consider the legacy from the English occupation to be quite useful. My friends in neighboring countries prize their French heritage. Yet only in rare and inspired moments did the white colonials and the black Africans ever approach a real partnership. Truly memorable moments occurred, as when individual blacks and individual whites learned to trust and respect each other. However, this exceptional behavior on the part of some enlightened individuals had little influence on colonial policy.

White masters did, however, impress upon black subjects the modern-day requirement for technology and know-how. And, upon occasion, foreign science and technology actually met endogenous African needs. I recognize the fine work in cocoa bean genetics and hybridizing done by the British authorities in Ghana and Nigeria. As a result, my country produces the best cocoa for the finest chocolate in the world—a superior grade included in the most prestigious European and American products.

Now that the frenzied, enormously hopeful, and ultimately catastrophic early years of African independence have entered history, and now that South Africans have begun to lance wounds that have festered since the bad old days and have started a healing process, all Africans can look forward to mutually beneficial dealings with friends throughout the continent and throughout the world. In my estimation, economic growth will progress best on a case-by-case basis, initiated within the private sector. But governmental, intergovernmental, and extragovernmental

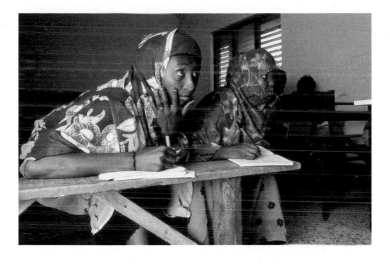

Africa's legendary oral culture— a treasure trove of spoken history, songs, and storytelling—is fertile ground for planting a modern information culture. And the populace is anxious to buy into that kind of future. Even as war raged in Somalia, some public schools managed to stay open (left, above). In the Democratic Republic of the Congo, radio stations (left, below) and other electronic media outlets spread information and provide training for the rising technology-savvy generation.

interventions are surely required to shatter the obstacles that stand in Africa's way. We have little margin for error. It is as if we must pass through the eye of a needle, or rather the eyes of many needles, to get from here to there. But in confronting these problems there is also great potential for harnessing Africans' inventive spirit.

Consider the issue of public health—public disease might be a better term—across the vast African continent. Studies by the World Health Organization indicate that in many African countries more than 20 percent of all children die before the age of five. An estimated 1.5 million children die each year from respiratory tract diseases such as pneumonia, whooping cough, and measles. Recent years have seen a great reduction in acute malnutrition of children, yet nearly 30 million girls and boys are underweight and about 40 million suffer from retarded development.

Diarrheal diseases bring death to perhaps two million children each year, and cholera lingers, posing a major threat to both children and adults. Death from tuberculosis knows no age limit. Malaria, the main cause for concern among the parasitic diseases, is becoming increasingly difficult to control. Nor are these alarming illnesses confined to rural areas; city dwellers are susceptible as well, and to the global scourge of HIV/AIDS.

Three-quarters of the more than 38 million people in the world with AIDS reside on the African continent. It is now the leading cause of death in Africa, surpassing age-old killers such as malaria,

The monumental stonework of 14th-century Great Zimbabwe astounded the first European visitors to southern Africa and still testifies to the sophistication of sub-Saharan civilizations. This African kingdom owed much of its prosperity to the skills of its metalworkers and its control of the flourishing gold trade.

Wisdom lies neither in fixity nor in change, but in the dialectic between the two.

—OCTAVIO PAZ

tuberculosis, and other infectious diseases. The joint international program UNAIDS estimated that at the end of the year 2005 nearly one thousand deaths were occurring daily due to AIDS in South Africa; five and a half million in that nation alone suffered from the disease. These statistics represent but one country. Yet a similar story can be told in many countries across the continent.

Without choosing to be, Africa has become a continent-wide laboratory for AIDS research. Traditional healers, using their knowledge of local flora to experiment with herbal treatments for AIDS, have had successes that are regrettably unknown outside of their communities at present. Ghanaian scientists working with healers have identified a number of herbs whose antiviral properties have successfully increased white blood cell counts and appear to reduce the viral load of HIV-infected cells.

Communication links developed in the 20th and 21st centuries will allow healers to share their expertise among their fellow Africans and with the world at large in a way they have never been able to before. I have always believed that the therapeutic value of plants will feature prominently in the search for new medical starting materials for the next generation of wonder drugs. The African continent, with its extensive biological diversity, should play a major role in the judicious exploitation of its resources.

My own research in medicinal plants over the past three decades has convinced me that the current high cost of treating HIV/AIDS patients through the administration of very expensive medications from the developed world can be dramatically reduced if researchers, particularly in Africa, can exploit the medical and nutritional value of the continent's native plants. This conviction may sound unusual, but for those in the developing world, where health delivery systems are based on traditional herbal treatments, the curative nature of these plants is well known.

HIV/AIDS experiments in my country involving traditional medical practitioners and highly trained modern Western medical research scientists indicate that there is tremendous potential in herbal preparations as early medical intervention for people who have tested HIV-positive. These initial indications have led my collaborators and me to speed up our efforts in screening our native plants for phytomedicine with regard to finding new ways of developing low-cost treatments for HIV/AIDS through the application of novel plant-based compounds.

I believe that most of our rural and urban peoples possess economic, cultural, and intellectual assets which are wasted or actually destroyed by the industrial development of today. Development might be more rightly described as the transition from one age into another, the dying age embodying many holdovers from the much despised era of ruthless colonial exploitation. As the old passes, African vitality can find a most welcome outlet in the electronic cottage industries of the new information revolution.

In the highly industrialized nations, building upon the new economics of microprocessors, some major industries are reversing the trend toward urbanization. While the forms of community development are vastly nontraditional, they are also wonderfully appropriate. I believe that Africa's traditional geometry—the combination of the village, the market-logistical network, and the tribal center—is far more efficient and functional than outside observers might have suspected. In fact, these age-old patterns are worthy models on which to base the African continent's future growth.

Instead of people being displaced so that they can travel to the machines, information can be instantly distributed to the places where people prefer to live, thus shifting the work to the suburban and rural areas. This is still a dream in Africa, but not a distant dream. People of the industrialized world are learning that the village tradition need not be displaced to make way for factories. With a tool like the microprocessor, there is no necessity to create human jungles in the form of high-density cities. In the space of a century, for instance, Germany has developed a form of suburban subassembly plant that could pass for a nicely landscaped neighborhood school or social center.

The village is one of Africa's most beloved and, until recently, strongest institutions. Today the village is beset with fallout from Africa's unchecked population growth, natural catastrophes, the rape of the environment, abominable governance at the national level, and a swarm of lesser devils. The village has deteriorated, becoming a place where people live too little and die too soon. But it still survives, and it holds the key to Africa's rebirth.

The implications of our present village tradition with respect to agricultural development and health are enormous. Traditional knowledge about horticulture, animal husbandry, and herbal medicine is ripe for transformation into information databases that are married to microprocessor communication networks. With the pertinent information instantly available, local people will be able to design decentralized and flexible service-delivery systems that are well adapted to local conditions and expectations.

With the introduction of the microprocessor and reliable communication links, our villages could quickly become corresponding members of great memory banks. Information would, at first, flow out of villages into cyber-repositories to be sifted and processed before it becomes available online in the languages spoken in each region. With training, villagers will be able to access practical support in the form of truly appropriate technology.

In today's world, computer chips and satellite hookups (even to the most remote and disadvantaged rural areas) can take the place of leather drumheads lashed to sections of hollow log. This last was the hardware of Africa's ancient contribution to wireless telegraphy, the "talking drums." These talking drums allowed people to communicate across great distances without any wires to connect them. Now Africans are once again communicating without wires, but the distances across which they can communicate with today's wireless technology span the globe.

Africans are quite adaptable to new ideas and goods, a fact many outsiders find surprising. They may have expected traditional people with so many conservative values to reject change. Not so. The highly recommended marriage of apparent opposites—ethnic lore with cutting-edge technology—is both practical and proactive, two necessary attributes for the rebirth of the region. As with the talking drums of yesteryear, Africans have a long history of overcoming handicaps through the inspired application of their innate abilities. My dream is that, befitting our history as the cradle of the human creative spirit, Africa will become once again a "giver" to world culture, a rich source rather than an impoverished recipient of new ideas and inventions.

Winds of Change

MICHAEL GARSTANG

Great rivers of air flow in the atmosphere, linking together ecosystems as far-flung and dissimilar as land and sea, desert and rain forest. Winds near the equator can carry air 25,000 miles around the globe in as little as 20 days. Within the air we breathe are some 120 chemical elements and compounds; winds are frequently burdened with minute particles of soil, dust, minerals, plant and organic material, sea salt, marine minerals, combustion products from burning forests and grasslands, as well as products of agriculture, industry, and other human activities. At times, volcanic eruptions shoot gases and dust into the air. There is a constant, minute rain of extraterrestrial dust as well. Each year, a billion tons of material are lofted from the Earth's surface by wind and carried around the world.

The main sources of windblown dust are the great deserts of the world's subtropical regions—most notably the Sahara. Photographs taken by U.S. astronauts reveal huge plumes of dust rising off these dry lands. About half of all the dust entering Earth's atmosphere comes off the west coast of Africa and is blown out across the North Atlantic, creating a distinct layer in the atmosphere known as the Saharan Dust Layer. Much of it is initially lifted off the ground by dust devils, small tornado-like vortices common in deserts and dry regions. I have seen as many as 30 dust devils spinning at once. They rise above the desert surface to altitudes of at least 500 meters, where they catch west-blowing winds and begin their journey.

Of course, what goes up eventually comes down, and this is where atmospheric scientists have made some of the most surprising discoveries.

Circumnavigating dust falls on ecosystems far and wide and changes them. Over many thousands of years, winds have moved so much dust that almost no soil can be attributed only to the local bedrock. This includes one of the richest ecosystems on Earth: the Amazon Basin rain forest, where some 22 chemical elements (including phosphate and potassium, critical elements for plant growth) come from Saharan dustfall. Such trace elements are essential to rain forest vegetation, but they are nearly absent in the leached, nutrient-poor soils. In low-lying parts of the basin, river flooding periodically replenishes the soil, but in the higher, drier terra firma forest, atmospheric dust from Africa supplies virtually all the life-sustaining nutrients.

As part of a NASA-sponsored project to study the role of tropical rain forests in Earth's interconnected life-sustaining systems, I and my colleagues sampled Saharan dust in the air over the Amazon Basin. From these measurements we estimated that each year the eastern and central Amazon Basin receives a shower of about 13 million tons of Saharan dust.

But the trade winds blowing across the Atlantic generally aren't strong enough to carry enough dust to account for the quantities we measured in the air and rainfall of the central Amazon. Once we discovered that all episodes of Saharan dust incursions to the central basin coincided with large rainfalls, we began to understand the connections.

The same powerful weather systems capable of bringing in larger-than-average amounts of moisture and producing the heavy Amazon rains are also capable of carrying larger-than-average amounts of dust over long distances. Any time the birth of one of these storm systems in the Amazon Basin coincided with a large plume of Saharan dust over the western tropical Atlantic,

As a Sahara dust devil rises (above), it injects specks of soil into the atmosphere. Carried west by trade winds, the dust crosses the Atlantic to South America's Amazon Basin (left), where airborne moisture condenses on the particles and falls as rain, adding nutrients to the leached rain forest soils.

great quantities of dust were sucked into the Amazon. When there were storms over the Amazon but no dust plume over the western tropical Atlantic, heavy rains would fall but without much dust. Thanks to the coincidence of two dissimilar events on opposite sides of the ocean—a desert dust storm and a rain forest storm system—the barren Sahara replenishes the lush Amazon forest.

Leave It to the School Children

GEORGE P. HORSE CAPTURE

The economic forces that brought a mining company to the Fort Belknap Reservation in Montana were indifferent to the A'aninin people's spiritual ties with their land. No laws existed to protect their sacred ground from desecration. Economics eventually sent the miners away again, but not before they had reduced a meaningful mountain to rubble.

Every summer we make our way westward from New York City, eventually reaching Montana and our home on the Fort Belknap Reservation. We don't actually have a house there, but it's our home anyway. This is where all our people live and are buried. Returning to Indian country from the East Coast is much anticipated throughout the year. Numerous work projects fill my briefcase, but somehow the excitement, children, grandchildren, and other relatives always fill the hours and days, and I eventually leave Montana with the work unfinished.

We know we are home when Snake Butte appears and the blue-gray silhouette of the Little Rocky Mountains rims the southern horizon— our connections to the Earth. We are home at last.

After a wonderful night's sleep we drive to Hays, past Three Buttes to the west, past the fields of wheat on one side and the prairie filled with running horses on the other, past Peoples Creek flowing from the west. Making my way over Carrywater Road in the Little Rocky Mountains, I long to see my son, Junior, his wife, Teresa, and all my grandchildren. Junior is off to a meeting when I arrive, and Teresa has taken my grandkids

to the creek for a swim, so I go to look for them. I drive up to Little Peoples Creek, toward St. Paul's Mission. I appreciate the beautiful stream that carved its way through the canyon eons ago. Our tribal government scooped out ponds in this gravel creek bed to make swimming holes for the children. The water is clear and cool—a good place to escape the hot summer sun. Several families are having picnics and cooling off near the creek. I soon pass the Sundance grounds and the Powwow grounds, then I realize I've gone too far, somehow missed my grandkids. I continue up the beautiful canyon, though, between the quaking ash trees lining the road.

Driving up this newly graded mountain road is pleasant after driving on the wild streets of New York. The air is sweet. All is peaceful and beautiful. The incline is constant and the scenery gorgeous, but I am full of dread as I anticipate the scene ahead. I know what is up here. I know what is not up here. And as I emerge from the trees, I can see ahead a raw, tortured wall of earth.

Devastation.

I am depressed as I view a once proud monument reduced to rubble. This is what open-pit

Photographed by Edward Curtis in the 19th century, the author's great-grandfather saw his sacred land crumble under the miner's shovel.

*The true past departs not, no truth or goodness realized by man ever dies, or can die;
but all is still here, and, recognized or not, lives and works through endless change.*

—THOMAS CARLYLE

mining does to a mountain; it profits only those who live far away from the damaged landscape.

Such severe damage brings tears to my eyes, rage in my heart. This is like tearing off the breasts of your mother, revealing carnage and pain inside. The last time here, I could see the massive earth-moving trucks driving back and forth, but it's quiet now. It's quiet because the mining company has filed for bankruptcy. The only reason that the rape has stopped is because the price of gold has dropped. All the federal and state agencies did not stop it, nor could the environmental and local Indian groups—Red Thunder and the Island Mountain Protectors. But the stock market did. We all know, though, that when the price of gold rises, miners will be back.

A breeze is blowing. I can see the long grass waving back and forth from where I stand. I stand here in the bright reservation sunshine with a darkened heart. Before me, in ruins, is what once was a beautiful mountain—home of thick grasses, colorful flowers, towering pine trees, a place of prayer for my people. Birds, insects, eagles—they all lived here. Now there is nothing, only death.

How did we allow this to occur? We are all thinking human beings—have we no decency or respect? Is the quest for gold and money all there is? Are these the ultimate forces of change?

When one considers the forces of change, it is easy to think of them in grand terms such as Manifest Destiny and agricultural inventions, but one must remember that forces affect people, that they change human beings. We are all the same, you know. We all have bodies and we all should have faces. I would like to show you the faces of my people, so you can understand the impact of forces on us, the American Indian people.

We are not newcomers. We have been on this hemisphere longer than any other humans. Estimates and theories place us here from 13,000 to 70,000 years ago. At intervals, scientists redefine their theories and come up with different dates, but at a minimum it would be safe to say that we have been here at least 13,000 years.

Unhappy with the way scientists have treated us—from physical anthropologists to archaeologists, and others—many Indian people have questioned the Bering Strait theory that the origin of the American Indian people begins with us crossing the Bering Strait and then populating the hemisphere. We have our own theories of origin. Some tribes believe they came from an opening in the earth, others believe they came from the sky, and some tribes, such as mine, have different beliefs.

Our story says it had rained for a long time, perhaps 40 days and 40 nights, until the Earth was covered with water. On the surface of this gigantic ocean was Turtle, and on its back were a number of animals, birds, and First Man. They drifted for a long time. Finally First Man said he did not want to do this anymore; they had to create a world so they could live in a proper way. He urged the animals to dive down to the ocean's bottom and get some mud for him.

So one by one they dove into the murky depths. First the muskrat, then the beaver, then others, but none was successful. Some were never seen again; others barely made it back. Finally a waterbird said it wanted to go. So at the urging of others, the animal dove down. It swam harder and deeper. Much time went by, and the people on the back of Turtle began to worry. They thought they had lost another member of their family.

Suddenly there was a splash on the ocean's surface. It was the little waterbird, struggling to

In the early 1900s a group of buffalo Indians rides toward the sacred mountains near Hays, Montana. Behind the riders meanders Little People's Creek—today little more than a tailings sluice for the mine.

make its way toward the others. It was exhausted. In its beak was a bit of earth. Joyously, they pulled the bird aboard and gratefully acknowledged its success. First Man took the soil in his hand and rolled it back and forth in a circular motion. Slowly the mud ball grew larger. From a small round ball it grew until it became the world. Turtle and crew made their way to land. They disembarked and began to populate the world.

This is our story of creation. To this day, in gratitude for the brave deed it performed, we do not kill and eat that waterbird, the mud hen.

In my mind, the Bering Strait theory and our origin story are not incompatible. The Bering Strait is just another landmark we passed on the way coming here. Our origins could be somewhere else. During our journey here, we passed the Bering Strait and other places.

There are many ways to learn about American Indians. One of the best ways is by studying their languages. The languages of the tribes have changed little over the centuries and can be grouped into many large families. In the Athapaskan family are Chipewyan, Sarsee, and other tribes, including Navajo and Apache. In the Algonquian family are Cree, Blackfeet, Sauk, Fox, Shawnee, Cheyenne, and others, including Arapaho and my tribe, at one time called Atsina. Some

Even while a thing is in the act of coming into existence,
some part of it has already ceased to be.

—MARCUS AURELIUS

tribes in the Siouan family are Crow, Mandan, and, of course, Sioux. In this group also are Assiniboine. Some scholars estimate that there were 600 languages spoken in North America before contact with Europeans. Studying these languages allows us to determine relationships between tribes and theorize about tribal migrations. It is said that the Algonquian language group, which includes the language spoken by Pocahontas, was one of the first to arrive in this country.

Fifty-two names have been given to my tribe over the years. In the early 1800s we were known as Atsina, which is said to be a Blackfeet word. The common name used today, and in our treaties, is Gros Ventre, a French term meaning big belly. The derivation of this name comes from a sign-language gesture where the hand moves down the chest and away from the body, denoting that we are Water Falls or Falls Indians. This refers to a spot on the Saskatchewan River where the early Canadian trappers first saw us. When the sign was used in a distant area, it was misinterpreted as "big belly." Similarly, Hidatsa people in North Dakota were also named Gros Ventre. Many believe we can never truly be ourselves until all these names are discarded and we reinstitute our tribal names. There is an effort within my tribe to restore our native name: A'aninin, the White Clay People.

Historical records indicate that in very early times our people came from northeast of Red River, which divides North Dakota and Minnesota. In around 1700, our tribe moved west and divided. Our group, A'aninin, went northwest, and the others, Arapaho, went west and south. We traveled and lived in the area between the north and south branches of the Saskatchewan River and were described by the first Europeans that saw us as "good buffalo-hunting

Indians." The estimate of our population in 1780 was 3,000 people.

Cree and Assiniboine, being allied with each other and commercial fur-trappers, obtained the gun before other tribes in the Northern Plains. Together they began to push westward against our tribe and others in the region. We could not defeat this coalition, so we tried to stop their source of supplies by burning three forts in Canada. In 1826 we moved southward into what would become Montana. Our numbers were estimated in 1806 at approximately 300 lodges, with 7 people per lodge or tipi.

Around this time, the tribes of the Northern Plains were exposed to foreign diseases, which decimated our populations. Smallpox ran rampant, causing immense mortality rates. Often 50 to 70 percent of the infected people died, primarily children and elders. When the foreigners actually arrived in our region, our traditional way of life was already nearing its end.

In spite of these changes, our tribe continued to be quite active. We engaged enemies on the Santa Fe Trail, trappers at Pierre's Hole in Idaho, and others across Montana. In 1833 German Prince Maximilian journeyed up the Missouri River. Our tribe met him where the Arrow River meets the Missouri River in Montana. Swiss artist Karl Bodmer painted images of some of our people at this meeting. In 1847 there were 230 lodges of our tribe.

It is said that the last great herd of buffalo lived in our area, but by 1885, excess hunting had nearly exterminated this herd. Our people debilitated by the effects of deadly diseases, and our movements restricted more and more by treaties, we were unable to sustain ourselves with buffalo. Our country, though, was described as "beautiful, level country, well covered with grass," and in 1876 our population was estimated at 960.

As the tribes were suffering from these changes, they were squeezed into smaller areas. Intertribal conflicts broke out more frequently as one tribe fought against another. To establish firm tribal boundaries, our present reservation was established by the Fort Belknap Agreement, ratified by Congress on May 1, 1888.

The reservation was named after President Grant's secretary of war, William Worth Belknap. He was impeached by Congress in 1876 for accepting bribes and resigned before the trial to avoid further disgrace. The reservation encompasses more than 600,000 acres in Blaine and Phillip Counties in Montana. It is rectangular in shape, 25 miles from east to west, with the long side going north and south for 40 miles.

The northern boundary is the Milk River, so named by Lewis and Clark because of its murky color. The southern boundary is the crest of the Little Rocky Mountains, which rise from the surrounding plains. We call them the Island Mountains or the Fur Cap Mountains. In this relatively small area there are three ecosystems: a river environment to the north, with cottonwood trees and irrigation capabilities; a mountainous area to the south, with rugged canyons, pine trees, and soaring eagles; and a rolling prairie, once covered with buffalo grass. This is where we now live. It is a beautiful reservation.

The tragedy of the mountains has taken many forms. One began long ago, during the mountain-building process of the Earth, before there were Indian people or miners. The intrusion of molten rock under this area created enough internal pressure to force the topmost layers of the Earth's crust upward into the shape of a dome,

capped by Madison limestone. The layers of this dome have eroded over the eons, creating spectacular canyons; the remains of the dome, our mountains, are covered with grasses, brush, and pine trees. The most important minerals in these mountains are of low-grade quality and include quartz, sericite, fluorite, sylvanite, and gold. The cursed gold.

Folk legends had it that the Indian people knew about the presence of the gold in the Little Rocky Mountains for a long period of time. The soft metal didn't fit within their lifestyle, so they didn't use it, but they soon realized that the Euro-Americans would do anything to get it. Accounts say that "upon pain of death," the Indian people were forbidden to reveal the location of the gold.

During and before our early settlement in the 1850s, the white people relentlessly continued their movement westward on their quest for Manifest Destiny, wreaking havoc with the landscape, razing anything that produced money. Few of them were able to really see what they were losing. Over the past hundred years, forests have been devastated for their lumber, rivers dammed to produce electricity, air polluted by factories, and people removed from their land. As the juggernaut churned its way West, the forces of change either destroyed or swept before them those entities or native people that God created. By the late 1880s, in the Northern Plains, the tribes were restricted to reservations. But the forces continued to pursue them even there.

Then another tragic force intervened. Mining laws were established long ago and continue to cause terrible damage today. The U.S. Congress passed the General Mining Law of 1872. This law, one of a series that encouraged people to go West, was originally intended to inspire prospectors. The law was generous, but only benefited a few.

It allowed developers the exclusive right to mine hard-rock minerals from federal or public lands. It implemented a system for claims that protected prospectors' discoveries from infringement by others, establishing that the finder of a valid claim could mine the minerals or "patent" the land as private property. So with their picks, shovels, and burros, prospectors sought the yellow riches, established settlements, and promoted the nation's Manifest Destiny.

The foreign intrusion began with French explorers, the Vérendryes, in 1743, and then Lewis and Clark from 1804 to 1806. Next came the fur traders, who arrived after Lewis and Clark; then cattlemen, after the rich grasslands of the Northern Plains; then miners, settlers, and others.

They followed the gold strikes: from California (forty-niners), then Colorado (fifty-niners), eventually making their way to Montana from the south. The first Montana gold strikes were near Drummond in the 1850s, then in 1862 at Grasshopper Creek. By 1866, Montana was the second highest producer of gold in the United States. Eventually miners heard about strikes in the Little Rocky Mountains, along the southern border of what became the Fort Belknap Reservation, and some made their way there. Although initially forbidden by law, miners crossed into the land anyway, setting up operations and panning for riches. Our population in 1883 was estimated at 970.

At first prospectors staked land claims. What earth scars they made were often concealed by foliage and pine trees. Later, companies using similar techniques mined on a larger scale. The riches attracted still others, and eventually the local, state, and congressional politicians bowed to the pressure of the numerous non-Indian constituents who demanded gold-bearing areas on Indian reservations be taken and mined by them. In response, the government commissioned William C. Pollock, Walter M. Clements, and George Bird Grinnell to meet with the Indian people and obtain their land.

Less than two weeks before the Fort Belknap proceedings, these same commissioners met with the Blackfeet and purchased for 1.5 million dollars a vast tract from the western edge of the Blackfeet reservation, where non-Indians could search for gold. It was 20 times as large as the proposed land sale on Fort Belknap. No worthwhile deposits were found, so the land became part of Glacier National Park. In the mid-1870s, Crow people suffered a massive land loss for the same reason.

On October 7, 1895, Pollock and Grinnell met with the Indian people. Comments of the commission and Indian people regarding the sale of the mountains were recorded for history in Senate Document 117, 54th Congress, Session 1:

White Weasel (Gros Ventre): "You commissioners have come to get part of the reservation, and I can't very well spare any of it. I don't like to sell it. I don't want to sell. That is all I can say." (White Weasel here touches the stenographer's pen in testimony of his statement.)

Sleeping Bear (Gros Ventre): "The Indians are talking all different and I don't know what to do, so I think I will not sell; that is all I can tell you. I can't sell any of the reservation."

Black Wolf (Gros Ventre): "I can't sell any of the reservation; the reservation is small enough now; I can't sell any of it." (Black Wolf here touches the pen in testimony of his statement.)

Jerry Running Fisher (Gros Ventre): "I am willing to sell a part of the reservation. I think

Boys will be boys: Kids living on Fort Belknap
Reservation fish and horseplay in the water, even
though gold mining has tainted their streams. In
2004 Montana voters approved a statewide ban
on open-pit cyanide leaching, and state funds now
go to fill pits and replant hillsides.

A wise man's question contains half the answer.

—SOLOMON IBN GABIROL

I will do well afterwards if I sell a part of the reservation."

Bushy Head (Gros Ventre): "I am willing to do as you men advised me. I would like to get more cattle; that is all."

Lame Bull (Gros Ventre): "Look at my hair; it is gray. I say the same thing as I said before— I don't want to sell."

Great-grandfather Horse Capture said, "I can't sell the reservation myself; I leave it to the school children."

At the end of the day Mr. Pollock told the Indians, in part:

We are sorry to find that you are not yet agreed… We told you on Saturday that we saw no way for you to get beef, cattle, flour, wagons or anything else after your present agreement expires, unless by the sale of some more of your land…. If the majority, the most of you, do not think this, all we can do is to go back to Washington without having done anything. If we do this and you come to the agent three years from now and ask him for something to eat, or for a wagon, or for some cattle, you will be very much disappointed when you cannot get it.

If, then, you go back to your women and babies without anything, and they are crying for something to eat, you will be sorry that you did not think better at this time.

Mr. Grinnell also spoke:

I see that some of you people are pretty blind; you can't see far…. You are like people looking through a fog—you see things near by, but the things far off are hidden…. I go about among different people and see them, how they are fixed, how many cattle they have got, how they farm; I don't see anybody as poor as you people.

"Two years from now," Mr. Grinnell told the Indians that day, "if you don't make any agreement with the Government, you will just have to kill your cattle and then you will have to starve."

The Senate document indicates that of 334 male adult Indians from the two tribes, 189, a majority, signed the agreement: about five-sixths of the Assiniboine and only one-quarter of the Gros Ventre. The tribes deeded away 40,000 acres of land and received $360,000—$9 per acre. On October 9, 1895, the Grinnell Agreement was completed, the land lost to governmental pressure, coercion, and betrayal. Funds due the Indians of Fort Belknap may never have reached them. The reservation agents of the time, Luke C. Hays and his successor, Morris L. Bridgeman, were later accused of fraud. Hays committed suicide before he could be indicted; Bridgeman was convicted of fraud and imprisoned.

That year, 1895, our tribal population was 596.

In 1979 the mountains began experiencing drastic, tragic change. Pegasus Gold of Canada, a mining conglomerate, entered into agreement with some western American subsidiaries and organized Zortman Mining. Together they ushered in a new era and a new mining technique—the cyanide heap-leach process, which allows profitable mining of very low-grade ore.

The mining process they established requires removing immense amounts of ore at low cost: First, bulldozers cut a road in the mountainside to the top. A flat working area is made by scraping off the soil to the bedrock. Next, a series of holes is drilled into the rock and explosives are inserted and detonated. The entire level is pulverized by the explosions. The heavy equipment moves in again and scrapes off the pulverized material, which is loaded into trucks and driven to a leach pad and dumped. When all the debris is removed, the area is once again scraped level, drilled, and exploded, and the rock is again pulverized and dumped onto the pad. Layer after layer is taken from the mountain.

The pulverized rock on the leach pad grows. Next it is saturated with a solution containing cyanide. As the liquid cyanide solution soaks through the debris and dissolves minerals, the gold flows toward the drains. Once the dissolving liquid reaches the plastic-lined bottom, it flows away from the pad in pipes to holding ponds. Later, the gold is removed. In this manner, huge amounts of mountain can be mined. According to the Billings *Gazette*, between 92 and 100 tons of rock are processed for each ounce of gold. The process mutilates the earth. It is like cutting down a forest to get a two-by-four piece of lumber.

In 1923 our estimated population was 586.

There are documented environmental problems associated with this heap-leach method. The leach pad's plastic lining, on which pulverized material is dumped, eventually tears from trucks driving over it. The cyanide seeps through the tears into the soil. Eventually it reaches groundwater.

Other materials in the pulverized heap become more susceptible to leaching and erosion. The heavy metals in them—arsenic, copper, lead, and zinc—disintegrate faster, because they are no longer embedded in a solid form. They drain downward when it rains. This is the real danger. When these drainages meet with sulfur-bearing minerals and air, they form sulfuric acid runoffs that kill fish and other living things.

Current monitoring of leach-pad drainage, open pits, waste rock, and tailings sites is inadequate and underfunded. State authorities cite budget cuts as the reason for not determining how dangerous the drainage areas are. It is difficult for the Indian people to conduct the tests; we lack the resources and equipment to do so. Periodically others have come to our assistance, but the test results have been sporadic and may vary drastically with changing weather conditions. The areas adjacent to the mining debris contain no vegetation; nothing lives in the water. But a little farther down the creek, the setting can look unchanged and natural. A high level of concern is difficult when everything seems normal to the observer.

Today a number of concerned organizations and individuals are objecting to the provisions of the General Mining Law of 1872, which still applies to all the patents and mining claims on 432 million acres of publicly owned land in the western United States. Among these organizations is the National Wildlife Federation, whose 1997 "Primer on the Mining Law of 1872" cited the following facts:

- Mining claims within national parks, national wildlife refuges, wild and scenic river and wilderness areas are still valid if made before area boundaries were established—an estimated total of 752 patents and 1,346 mining claims.
- Mining companies pay no rent, severance tax, or royalty for mineral extraction; they can lease their claims to other miners and collect royalties.
- The law does not allow the federal government to determine when mining is an inappropriate use of public lands, nor does it address the impact of mining on the environment or require that the areas affected by mining be reclaimed after operations have ceased.

Ancient spirits move a dancer during Milk River Indian Days, an annual celebration among the Assiniboine and Gros Ventre Indians living at Fort Belknap Reservation.

The agencies that administer public land, the Bureau of Land Management and the Forest Service, have inadequate regulations for environmental protection and reclamation; they generally defer to the policies implemented by state governments. In 1988 the General Accounting Office estimated that 232,000 acres needed to be reclaimed as a result of mining, and that over 235 million dollars were needed for reclamation. That was nearly 20 years ago.

There is one last great danger of hard-rock mining: This procedure means the removal of a mountain made by God. It is like removing the sky and the clouds. All these things form a part of our universe, and they form a balance with each other, and with us. Without them we are incomplete.

I traveled down the mountain road, saddened by historical events that I live with, that haunt my people. Driving off the main road, I did eventually find my grandchildren. They were happily splashing away in a pond, oblivious to everything except being children.

Later, after talking with my wife, and after carefully looking at a map, I realized something. I found that the waters of the north fork, the middle fork, and the south fork, as well as South Big Horn Creek and King Creek, all eventually come together in Little Peoples Creek. King Creek begins at the foot of the Gold Bug Butte mine waste. Aided by gravity, the dissolved poisons flow downward to our reservation, past the Powwow grounds, past the Sundance grounds, down the canyon, and into the ponds—into the beloved waters where my grandchildren play.

In our tribal culture, the most important way to communicate with the One Above and to become a man in our world is through a vision quest, which always takes place on a mountain. The questor climbs a prominent butte or mountain and fashions the rocks around himself in order to build a sort of mountaintop nest. With his pipe, his tobacco, and his buffalo robe, he fasts for four days and nights. During that time, he is praying to God and contemplating his life and the universe.

Having some understanding of the nature of the American Indian's spiritual mind, I am certain that all the peaks in the Little Rocky Mountains have been fasted upon during a vision quest at one time or another. Just because the oral tradition of the Indian does not record the names of the mountains upon which they fasted, it does not mean that men at one time or another did not pray on them. All of these mountains are sacred—and now they are being removed for gold.

The remnants of our two sacred mountains can still be seen in the Little Rocky Mountains. But how can a mountain that has been ravished by open-pit mining be reclaimed? Perhaps by throwing grass seed in the holes that remain.

As Giant Turtle enters the new millennium, a point in our history is marked—the perfect time to pause, look back at our values, mining laws, policies, and actions, honestly evaluating what has been done. We must realize that our world is finite, our resources have limitations. What may have been acceptable for one era may not best serve another. We must make changes for the future. Let's do it now; it means changing mining laws ... and leaving our Earth to the school children.

Our tribal population—those living on or near the reservation with one-quarter or more A'aninin blood—is now 3,088.

Deadly Walls of Water

TOM O'NEILL

On December 26, 2004, it was as if a bomb had exploded on the ocean floor—or, to be more precise, 23,000 atomic bombs, all the size of the one dropped on Hiroshima.

Beneath the Indian Ocean, two tectonic plates—the vast, sliding sheets of Earth's crust that carry the continents and the oceans—had been rubbing each other the wrong way for 40 million years. The plates had collided, with one being forced under the other, causing the edge of the top plate to bend backwards. When the top plate finally sprung free, the result was one of the most massive earthquakes in recorded history. A similar collision involving these plates raised the Himalaya long ago.

The mega-atomic force sent billions of tons of water rocketing outward from the epicenter at a speed of more than 500 miles per hour. NASA reported that the earthquake actually made the Earth spin faster and wobble in orbit. All anyone noticed, though, were the colossal waves that swamped shorelines from Thailand to Africa.

Those towering walls of water are the result of water striking land. A tsunami barely ripples the ocean's surface in deep water. But as the wave rolls into shallow coastal water, the front slows down while the back of the wave is still traveling with the speed of a jet airliner. The result is a tidal pile-up known as amplification—the back of the wave catches up with the front as the wave collides with the shoreline.

Just 155 miles from the epicenter of the earthquake, Sumatra was the first hit. It felt the full force of the tsunami, with an estimated 100,000 tons of water coming ashore for every meter of coastline. Three-quarters of all the tsunami's victims were in Sumatra. More than 1,800 people were drowned or crushed by debris in Khao Lak, Thailand, where the wall of water tore through huts and hotels almost two hours after the time of the quake. The tidal wave continued on, devastating Sri Lanka and the Maldives, more than a thousand miles away from the epicenter.

Warning came too late or not at all. The count of dead and missing climbed over 300,000, and millions more lost homes and livelihoods in more than a dozen countries throughout the Indian Ocean. Many of the communities hit had virtually no memory of a powerful tsunami or what the warning signs of an approaching one would be—the last oceanwide wave, from the eruption of Krakatau off southern Sumatra, occurred in 1883. Lacking that knowledge and any kind of detection or warning systems in the Indian Ocean, coastal areas were defenseless against the waves.

With tectonic plates groaning against each other or pullling apart on every ocean floor, the risks of large submarine quakes and resulting tsunamis have galvanized scientists and planners to prepare for the next onslaught. Since 1992, 17 major tsunamis have struck, 11 in the Pacific. Fatalities were relatively low, a total of some 4,000—until December 2004.

Burgeoning coastal populations have multiplied the human costs of a wave strike. To forestall another catastrophe, world leaders have agreed to work together to increase the existing network of underwater sensors in the Pacific, site of 85 percent of all tsunamis, and to expand the system into the Atlantic and Caribbean. Environmentalists, pushing for a further line of defense, look to nature itself and urge the planting of more mangrove forests as wave barriers.

Sending missives of hope heavenward (above), survivors released candle balloons during a mass prayer for the tsunami victims in Thailand's town of Takua Pa on January 19, 2005. Meanwhile, rescue and repair proceeded (below) as work elephants, managed by the Indonesian Ministry of Forestry, removed debris from otherwise inaccessible areas of the devastated terrain of Banda Aceh.

Biodiversity and Happiness

GRETCHEN C. DAILY

It is easy to forget that even in the 21st century, human societies
are sustained by natural ecosystems, often in ways not completely
understood. We need to find new methods of accounting for
the services nature provides, beyond the usual economic indexes.
What we take for granted today, we may lose tomorrow.

My dad says that the key to happiness in life is making sure you can always see something good on the horizon—being able to imagine with excitement an upcoming event and open possibilities for the future. When I was a child, the horizon was defined by the school year's end and the time remaining until our family's summer vacation at Fallen Leaf Lake.

All year long I would dream of getting ice cream from the little store down at the end of the lake, of taking a boat over glassy, smooth water in the early morning hours, and of how many crawdads I'd catch with a piece of Italian salami. Things didn't always work out as expected, but the mishaps were relatively minor and bonded the family together. With pangs of nostalgia, we still tell and retell stories about "the year we hiked into a hornet's nest," "the year the boat sank," and "the year Mrs. G.'s bathing-suit top flew off while she was waterskiing." Summers —the horizon—seemed to radiate with unplanned possibilities and adventure, which I enthusiastically looked forward to each year.

When I was older, my family moved to Europe, and the horizon took on new, broader dimensions. During school breaks we'd pack up the rusty old Volvo and strike out to explore new territory with little more than a road map and an English-something dictionary in hand.

Now—like most people's, I'm sure—my sense of well-being is quite sensitively tuned to the time horizon. It's nice to glance up from a busy day's work and feel a tinge of excitement for plans ahead: a cool evening run in the hills, a reunion with a good friend. While one's individual fate is inherently somewhat unpredictable, the key to peace of mind is a feeling of assurance and optimism that good things lie ahead.

In this respect, something unsettling is happening. For those watching nature's horizon closely, both assurance and optimism are fading. For most of human history, people have lived as their great-grandparents did; the horizon changed slowly, and the landscape itself remained essentially fixed. Today the very realm of possibilities is changing so quickly that even within one human lifetime, it is difficult to plot an imaginary course into the future.

And optimism is diminishing. So many of today's changes seem to be in the wrong direction.

Eighteenth-century naturalist Joseph Banks's collection of beetles only begins to display the vast range of species within just this single order of insects.

Let us a little permit Nature to take her own way;
she better understands her own affairs than we.

—MONTAIGNE

Until recently, the widespread faith that each generation would enjoy greater prosperity has characterized life in America. Yet while U.S. per-capita income was doubling between 1957 and 1992, the proportion of people reporting that they were "very happy" actually declined from 35 to 32 percent. Although the decline might not be significant, there was certainly no increase associated with economic growth.

Similarly, the Fordham Institute for Innovation in Social Policy calculated that, though real incomes increased by more than a third between 1970 and 1994, the Index of Social Health declined by 50 percent during the same period. Cherished aspects of the American Dream—like summer vacations on a pristine lake—seem to be receding from the reach of many. Contributing to such trends are profound environmental transformations that compromise the natural basis upon which economic prosperity depends. Still, there are promising signs on the horizon that indicate how we can better direct the course of these changes.

I suppose that ever since human beings evolved, people have been pondering what it is that makes us unique. Philosophers, religious leaders, poets, and plenty of ordinary people have had something to say about the topic. Some have extolled our virtues, proposing as unique our extraordinary intelligence; our development and use of tools; our complex communication systems, intricate social organization, intense feelings of love, and acts of loyalty and altruism. Others, lamenting our fall from grace, have pointed to betrayal, infanticide, and our genocidal tendencies. With deepening understanding of the natural world, we have come to appreciate that other organisms have beaten us on all of these traits; although we might stand out in some degree, we

aren't the evolutionary superstar we would like to think we were.

What does distinguish our species from all the others today, though, is the impact we have on the planet: *Homo sapiens* is one of perhaps 30 million species on Earth, yet it controls a disproportionate and rapidly growing share of the planet's resources. The human population numbered only about five million at the dawn of agriculture and grew very, very slowly over virtually all of human history to reach a billion people around 1800. Since then, billions have been added, in record time: In only 123 years, the second billion was added; in 33 years, the third; in 14 and 13 years, the fourth and fifth billion; recently, in a mere 12 years, the population on Earth reached six billion.

With the force of sheer numbers come other impacts unrivaled by any other species. Humans beings have:

- massively altered the biogeochemical cycles of major elements such as carbon, nitrogen, and sulfur, with dramatic changes in the chemical composition of the atmosphere, water, and soils;
- transformed minerals such as coal, oil, and metal ores from Earth's crust at rates that rival or exceed geological rates;
- dispersed millions of tons of synthetic chemicals annually while introducing 1,000 new ones per year to the approximately 100,000 now in the environment;
- converted vast tracts of diverse natural forest and grassland to uniform, managed forest, pasture, and food crops, greatly contracting the range of most wild species;
- inadvertently transferred species around the world while blocking (with highways, farm fields, and suburban sprawl) natural processes of dispersal.

In a sealed Kennedy Space Center chamber, scientists grow crops in a hydroponic environment with carefully monitored levels of nourishment, water, and oxygen. Aimed at developing space-bound agriculture, their work demonstrates how difficult it is to duplicate the delicate self-perpetuating biosphere that envelops planet Earth.

Among the potential consequences of these impacts are the decline in sperm counts in humans and disruption of the reproductive systems of many other species; rapid climate change threatening food production, access to fresh water, and low-lying coastal area security; and a mass extinction comparable to the one that wiped out the dinosaurs. Humanity has unwittingly changed virtually every cubic centimeter of the biosphere.

As dramatic as these changes are, we cannot see most of them with the naked eye. Without the aid of scientific instrumentation, complex analysis, and computer graphical display, one cannot grasp the enormity of these changes to the planet and to life on Earth—that is, the great impact on all life-forms set in motion when we migrated out of our African homeland, perhaps just 50,000 years ago,

and into virtually every other environment on the planet. And what we can't see, we tend to ignore.

Stanford biologist Paul Ehrlich likes to point out that, as sight-oriented creatures, we tend to be more disturbed by roadside litter than by much more serious, long-range threats to our health, homes, and lives, such as pesticide residues on food, contamination of drinking water, and other carcinogens in our immediate environment. If we tasted our way through life, as many organisms do, we'd have a keener sense of the environmental changes going on around us than we do with our big eyes and dull chemosensory abilities. Adding to our sensory limitations and biases, we seem more inclined to point our technological innovations and powers toward the heavens than toward our earthly surroundings. As Oxford

Airplanes spray insecticides over Fort Myers, Florida, to suppress the unwanted mosquito population. But they also kill butterflies and other insects that have positive effects on the area's plants and wildlife.

> *Not everything that can be counted counts,*
> *and not everything that counts can be counted.*
>
> —ALBERT EINSTEIN

biologist Robert May has noted, "Our catalogues of stars are more complete (by any reasonable measure), and vastly better funded, than catalogues of Earth's biota."

What do we know about the richness of Earth's biota and changes therein? Let's start by defining biodiversity: It is the full variety of life at all levels of organization, from variation in the molecular sequences of genes to that among distinct populations of a species to that among whole ecosystems, such as rain forests and arctic tundra. Although debates still rage over the precise definition of a species, biologists tend to focus on the species level when characterizing biodiversity. Diversity at the other levels is extremely important, both scientifically and economically, but is much more difficult still to quantify.

To date, taxonomists have named about 1.8 million species, yet even a simple statistic like this is not certain. There is no central species catalogue, and different museums are often found to have the same species registered under different names. Nonetheless, this 1.8 million must be seen as a very conservative number. Only a small fraction of Earth's tiniest creatures—insects, arachnids, crustaceans, fungi, microorganisms, and so on— are known, in spite of their paramount roles in running the show on Earth. Even in the best known groups (those that are the easiest to see, and the warmest and cutest among them such as birds and mammals), new discoveries continue to be made—about two to three new bird species per year and about one new mammal genus (typically containing several species) per year. So what's the grand total? Estimates range from 7 to 80 million species, yet most methods of extrapolation (which ignore many microorganisms) yield estimates toward the lower end of this range.

But today our activities threaten to drive Earth's biological diversity to its lowest level in human history. Harvard biologist E. O. Wilson calls this the folly our descendants are least likely to forgive us. Biodiversity was at its highest level when human beings first appeared on Earth. Of course, species have always come and gone—no one is here forever—but today extinction rates are thought to be at least a hundred to a thousand times faster than natural background rates.

In the past 2,000 years, 20 percent of Earth's bird species were driven to extinction by human activities. Of the extant fauna of today, 11 percent of birds, 25 percent of mammals, 20 percent of reptiles, 25 percent of amphibians, and 34 percent of fish appear to be on the brink of extinction. A conservative estimate of the rate of species loss globally is around three per hour. This corresponds to an estimated loss of 2,700 distinct populations per hour, according to Stanford biologist Jennifer Hughes and colleagues. The rate of loss for populations is much higher than the rate of loss for species. Lion populations, for instance, once inhabited land from Africa to the Indian subcontinent, but today they are restricted to a tiny fraction of their original range, mostly to a few game reserves in Africa. Population diversity begins to erode long before the very last individual of a species perishes.

What are the societal consequences of extinction? I find it helpful to begin thinking about the importance of Earth's biodiversity by way of a thought experiment, proposed originally by Harvard physicist John Holdren.

Imagine that a year from today, you will step into a spaceship and embark on a one-way trip to the moon. Let's assume for the sake of argument that the moon, miraculously, already has some of the basic conditions for supporting human life, such as an atmosphere, a climate, and a physical soil structure similar to that on Earth. After coaxing your family and friends into coming along, and packing your prized possessions, the big question would be: Of all of Earth's millions of species, which would you need to make the sterile moonscape habitable?

You could first choose from among all the species on Earth used directly in food, drink, spices, fiber, timber, pharmaceuticals, and industrial products such as waxes, rubber, fragrances, and oils. Oxford biologist Norman Myers has made a wonderful catalogue of these. Even being selective, this list could amount to hundreds or even thousands of species—and you still would not have begun considering the species needed to support and maintain life: the bacteria, fungi, and invertebrates that recycle wastes and maintain soil fertility; the insects, bats, and birds that pollinate flowers; and the herbs, shrubs, and trees that hold soil in place, nourish animals, and help control the gaseous composition of the atmosphere that influences Earth's climate.

No one knows exactly how many species, nor which combinations, would be required to support human life. So rather than listing individual species, you would do better to sketch out the life-support services required for survival on your lunar colony. A partial list of the necessary services would include:

- production of a wide variety of ecosystem goods such as seafood, timber, forage, and many pharmaceuticals
- purification of air and water
- protection against natural disasters such as flood and drought

- detoxification and decomposition of wastes and cycling of nutrients
- generation and preservation of soils, renewal of soil fertility
- pollination of crops and natural vegetation
- dispersal of seeds
- control of the vast majority of agricultural pests
- maintenance of biodiversity
- protection from the sun's harmful ultraviolet rays
- partial stabilization of climate
- provision of aesthetic beauty and intellectual stimulation.

These benefits, collectively called ecosystem services, are the conditions and processes through which natural ecosystems, and the species that are a part of them, sustain and fulfill human life.

Selecting the species to bring with you to supply these services is not a task you'd want to defer until your last Sunday afternoon on Earth. Take soil fertility as an example. Soil organisms play crucial roles in maintaining soil fertility, and all higher plants (including croplands, gardens, beautiful landscapes) depend on them. The abundance of soil organisms is absolutely staggering: Under a square yard of pasture in Denmark, for instance, just the top two inches of soil was found to be inhabited by roughly 50,000 small earthworms and their relatives, 50,000 insects and mites, and nearly 12 million roundworms. Just before the scientists cataloguing this stuff went blind, they decided to take a close look at the microorganisms in a pinch (one gram) of this soil. In it they found an estimated 30,000 protozoa, 50,000 algae, 400,000 fungi, and billions of individual bacteria of unknown numbers of species. Which should you choose to bring to the moon?

The task is not necessarily easier in the case of known species—those that have been given names.

Entering an alpine forget-me-not on a Colorado ridge, an ant pollinates the plant, performing an essential task for the flower's reproductive process. Not only bees, butterflies, and ants pollinate: Bats, birds, and other creatures all play roles as plants find sometimes surprising allies to help perpetuate their species.

The species name on its own is no more helpful than a company name in the white pages of a phone book. Without the yellow pages—some minimal information on what these species do, with whom and how they interact—you would have little way of judging whether you were bringing on board: a tree adapted to hot and dry or to cool and moist conditions; a tasty crop or a noxious weed; a valuable insect pollinator or a vector of disease.

Even with a year to plan the trip, packing would be difficult! Think of pollination services, for instance. Pollinators are important for the production of more than 150 food crops in the United States, ranging from almonds, apples, and alfalfa to melons, plums, and squashes. Considering the proportions in which these crops are consumed, experts estimate that about one in three mouthfuls of food is produced with the aid of animal pollinators. But there are over 100,000 known pollinator species, each with its own special capabilities and requirements: different kinds of bats, bees, beetles, birds, butterflies, flies, and so on. Which to bring to the moon?

The same difficulty pertains in pest control. About 25 to 50 percent of the world's crop production is destroyed by pests annually. Fortunately, an estimated 99 percent of potential crop pests are controlled by natural enemies. But here again, knowing who the combatants are, which pest enemy is going for which pest, is crucial. Because of the deleterious effects of chemical pesticides, scientists are seeking better natural pest management strategies and are beginning to understand the players and their interactions. For life on the moon, these considerations argue for insurance: In other words, you would probably want to bring more species with you than the bare minimum.

The closest attempt at our life-on-the-moon experiment on Earth was the first version of the experiment called Biosphere II. In it, a facility constructed on 3.15 acres in Arizona sealed off its inhabitants as much as possible from the outside world. Eight people were meant to live inside for two years without the transfer of materials in or out. The system was fueled with sunlight (through transparent walls) and electricity (at a cost of about a million dollars per year).

As in the lunar colony, the experimenters had to decide which species should populate the closed ecosystem. Rather than fret over soil organisms, they simply hauled in tons of rich California soil and with it, they hoped, a wide array of fungi, arthropods, worms, and microorganisms. Then they added groups of other animals and plants. At the start, Biosphere II featured agricultural land as well as elements from an ambitious variety of natural ecosystems, such as tropical forest, savanna, marshland, desert, and even a miniature ocean with a miniature coral reef.

In spite of an investment of 200 million dollars in the design, construction, and operation of this model Earth, Biosphere II proved unable to supply the material and physical needs for the survival of the eight Biospherians. To put it mildly, many unexpected and unpleasant problems arose:

- Oxygen concentration dropped from 21 to 14 percent (a level normally found at 17,500-foot elevations), and carbon dioxide levels sky-rocketed, with large daily and seasonal fluctuations, making it very difficult for the Biospherians to breathe.
- Nitrous oxide concentrations rose to levels at which brain function can be impaired.

A hidden connection is stronger than an obvious one.

—HERACLEITUS

- Of 25 vertebrate species, 19 soon became extinct.
- All pollinators rapidly became extinct, thereby dooming to eventual extinction the majority of the plant species.
- There were population explosions of crazy ants and overgrowth of areas by aggressive vines and algal mats.
- Water purification systems failed.

Ecosystem services operate on such a grand scale and in such intricate and little explored ways, most cannot be replaced on the scale required by innovation and technology. The bottom line of the Biosphere II experiment is that there exists no demonstrated alternative to maintaining the viability of Biosphere I—our Earth.

For millions or billions of years before humanity came into being, interdependent ecosystem services have been supporting and sustaining a biologically diverse Earth. It is easy to overlook the intricate connections between ecosystems, and easy to take them for granted. Disrupting them beyond repair has been a long-range outcome that, until the late 20th century, was unfathomable.

Yet destructive impacts of human activities on natural ecosystems have escalated and globally imperiled biodiversity and ecosystem service delivery: Pollination, pest control, water purification, flood- and erosion-control services have all been seriously impaired, often at great economic cost.

How do we begin the task of protecting the ecosystems that provide us with these services? First, we must recognize that natural ecosystems and their biodiversity are capital assets which, if properly managed, will yield important life-support benefits over time.

A forest ecosystem, for instance, may supply water purification, flood control, pest control, and other services along with the production of goods such as timber and pharmaceutical products. Relative to physical capital (buildings, equipment, etc.), human capital (skills, knowledge, health), or financial capital (readily tradeable assets in a growing array of forms), natural capital is poorly understood, little valued, scarcely monitored, and undergoing rapid depletion. Up until now, there has been little incentive to measure or manage natural capital. It has been treated as essentially inexhaustible.

Sustainable management of ecosystem services will require an innovative approach. To begin, we need to identify ecosystems' basic components—their service networks—so that we know what is in Earth's ecosystem yellow pages. Next, we need to understand how the services operate on different levels—physical, biological, economic, and cultural. And, finally, we need to establish financial mechanisms and social institutions to monitor and safeguard them.

Characterizing ecosystem assets thus involves an explicit cataloguing of important services at a variety of scales. At the broadest level, it addresses these questions: Which ecosystems supply what services? For a given location, which are supplied locally, which are imported from elsewhere, and which are exported? Characterization involves finding answers to other questions as well, such as:

- What is the impact of alternative human activities (e.g., agriculture, forestry, industry) on the supply of services?
- How interdependent are the services? How does exploiting or damaging one influence the functioning of the others?

- To what extent, and over what time scale, are the services amenable to repair?
- Where do critical thresholds lie?
- How effectively, and at how large a scale, can existing or foreseeable technologies substitute for ecosystem services?
- What would be the social benefits and costs of managing ecosystem assets (e.g., land and water) in different ways?
- Given the current state of technology and scale of the human enterprise, how much natural habitat and biodiversity are required to sustain the delivery of ecosystem services locally, regionally, and globally?

Finally, characterization involves assigning some measure of importance, or value, to the services that are supplying benefits to society. Be it biological, aesthetic, or spiritual, no general, widely applicable methodology for doing this exists. It is important to emphasize that for the diverse human cultures across the globe, different types of services will require different valuation approaches. More important than valuation itself, however, is the development of institutions that will safeguard ecosystem services into the next millennium and beyond by rewarding their stewards.

Around the world, unique ways of capturing ecosystem service values, and rewarding economically those who safeguard them, are appearing. In parts of Zimbabwe, cattle ranchers are now finding ecotourism so lucrative that it pays to remove their livestock (and no cattleman does this lightly!) and to reestablish native game and other wildlife on their land for safari purposes.

In Napa Valley, California, local residents are dismantling failed hydroengineering structures and returning to natural flood-control mechanisms of the river—that is, natural wetland areas.

In the wheat belt of western Australia, farmers are restoring some farm fields to native habitat because they find this to be the most profitable way of restoring the hydrological balance on the cultivated land; this balance is maintained by deeply rooted native plants that keep destructive salts below the rooting zone of the wheat.

In Costa Rica, a large orange juice company is purchasing the local ecosystem services it needs (water supply, pest control, pollination, and orange peel disposal) from a natural protected area near the company. In Vietnam, community education and development projects have resulted in sustainable harvest of goods and services from a forest reserve that had been undergoing rapid degradation. And, finally, there is renewed interest in the diverse array of social institutions created by local indigenous communities to manage sustainably the harvest of ecosystem goods and services.

We are beginning to see on the horizon a growing understanding of the interdependence of human societies on natural resources. We also see the emergence of a wide array of innovative, locally tailored approaches for capturing ecosystem service values so that our individual immediate needs are aligned with society's long-term well-being. So far these changes amount to a faint glimmer on the horizon; they are occurring on a very small scale relative to what is required. But they provide an important beacon for where we need to go. They also supply important experiments for determining what does and doesn't work for striking out into new territory and, through trial and error and a good dose of common sense and cooperation, for charting a promising course for the future.

To Quench the Thirst of Cities

GRETCHEN C. DAILY

New York City's water was once considered so pure and salubrious that it was bottled and sold throughout the Northeast. It came from the Catskill Mountains, about a hundred miles to the north, and owed its high quality to the natural purification system of the Catskills' streams and woodlands. But in recent years, as development increased in the Catskill area, the natural system became degraded by sewage and agricultural runoff. The United States Environmental Protection Agency (EPA) stepped in, requiring that the city prove it could protect the watershed or face a federal order to build a filtration plant.

At first city administrators considered building the water filtration plant, but when they found that it could cost up to eight billion dollars, plus 300 million dollars each year in operating costs, they turned to an alternative solution, namely restoring and safeguarding the natural purification system of the Catskills. This meant buying land in and around the Catskill watershed, as well as subsidizing upgrades to local sewage treatment plants, improving farming practices, and initiating environmentally sound economic development. The estimated cost of this option was 1.5 billion dollars. The city floated an Environmental Bond Issue to fund the watershed protection plan.

The Catskills supply many other valuable environmental services. Their natural habitats help control floods, mitigate the buildup of greenhouse gases by absorbing carbon dioxide, and—perhaps above all—give people a place where they can find beauty, serenity, and inspiration. These benefits reach other populations, animal and otherwise. It would be absurd to try to express the full ecosystem service value of the Catskills in a dollar figure. In this case, fortunately, there was no reason to try: Even a conservative estimate of the value of the natural asset was sufficient to induce adoption of a conservation policy.

The challenge today is to extend this model to other communities and to other kinds of ecosystem services. The EPA recently estimated that treating, storing, and delivering safe drinking water throughout the United States over the next 20 years without the benefit of natural capital would require an investment in physical capital of 140 billion dollars. Currently, more than 140 municipalities in the United States are considering watershed protection as a more cost-effective option than building artificial treatment facilities. This option is especially appealing because it aligns market forces with the environment, meaning that the short-term economic incentives for individuals are in accord with long-term social well-being.

For example, Rio de Janeiro and Buenos Aires, both with highly threatened watersheds of enormous biotic value, are investigating such an option. Costa Rica, which derives 99 percent of its electricity from hydroelectric plants, uses water from protected watershed areas to generate electricity. In 1995 Costa Rica established a small tax on water and electricity use, the revenues

New York City has long gotten most of its drinking water from sources in the distant Catskill Mountains (above), brought to the city through miles of pipelines (left). In response to new requirements, the city was faced with the choice of filtering some 1.2 million gallons of drinking water each day or developing a comprehensive water-quality protection strategy. It soon became apparent that addressing the source of the problem, rather than just its symptoms, was the most economical option. The city has implemented a program of land purchase and management to restore nature's own purification system.

from which are now recycled into managing the protected areas to limit erosion and sedimentation and to maintain high water flows. As in the Catskills, the plan will provide numerous ancillary benefits, including flood control, biodiversity conservation, and opportunities for ecotourism.

According to Walter Reid of the World Resources Institute, there is sufficient potential for safeguarding a whole suite of economically important watershed services to justify pursuing this option worldwide. Of course the feasibility of watershed protection for drinking water supply will vary by geographic region, with ecological, economic, and political circumstances. Reid estimated that in the United States, about three-quarters of an acre per person on average is needed to sustain a supply of safe drinking water. This amounts to 10 percent of the country's land area—a significant fraction. Extrapolating his calculations to the world yields an even cruder, but nonetheless illuminating, estimate—to sustain a supply of safe drinking water, watershed protection measures would have to extend over 13 percent of world land area under the current population size, and 23 percent of land area under a projected future population size of ten billion. Managing this amount of land for water purity would require a major commitment but, if done strategically, could be amply repaid in securing other critical ingredients for human well-being and economic prosperity.

Lava formed these cliffs in Oregon; now the waters of Vidae Falls help sculpt their shape. They also support some 600 plant species, including hot pink penstemon blossoms.

Afterword

ROBERT FRI

Natural History and the 21st Century

L iving successfully in a world shaped by powerful forces of change is not easy—but then it never was. Change has been constant for more than four billion years, and the ability to cope successfully with change is what characterizes our planet and life on Earth. What is new is that humanity itself has become a profound force of change. And so the question has become whether we can manage this force—that is, our own actions, views, and policies—so that future generations will have the options they need to develop fully. Or will our generation so deplete the Earth's resources that our descendants must live poorer, more brutish lives than we?

Our preference so far has been for consumption rather than self-control. We enjoy material prosperity and the personal convenience, comfort, and choice that come with it. In its pursuit, we seek to draw from the natural world the resources that make prosperity possible. To preserve the good life, we have even learned to control our environment to compensate for, and sometimes to resist, the natural forces of change.

Humanity is a force of change that is not likely to abate any time soon. Only a few of us are really comfortable with curtailments on our acquisitiveness or are content to live simply, with minimum necessities. Most of us are not, and continue to aspire to greater prosperity. Unfortunately, the latter group is both larger and growing far more quickly than the former, and the resulting pressure on the natural world is mounting rapidly—and is believed to be unsustainable. It is this concern that is at the core of the current sustainable development debate, one that began when the World Commission on Environment and Development first introduced the term in its 1987 seminal report. The report defined sustainable development as the ability "to meet the needs of the present without compromising the ability of future generations to meet their own needs."

Rings painted on oak bamboo branches in Costa Rica will tell ecologists the plant's rate of growth.

Steam, smoke, and clouds mingle in
Vancouver, Canada. Similarly difficult
to distinguish are civilization's effects
on environment.

The notion of unsustainablity—that the planet's resources will someday run dry—
is among the most venerable of policy arguments on economic development. Indeed, in
his classic 1798 "Essay on the Principle of Population," the English economist and cleric
Thomas Malthus advanced the first modern prediction of unsustainable development. He
argued that the demand for food to support a growing population in industrializing
England would ultimately outrun the available food supply. The inevitable consequence
of his thesis was a population that, over the long term, could exist only at subsistence
food-supply levels.

Malthus turned out to be famously wrong—though not entirely, for it is only
our species that has figured out how to control nature to increase food
supplies. Today people in every developed country worry more about too
many rather than too few calories. Malthus, however, was not alone. For the past couple
of centuries other doomsayers have issued numerous warnings that the world is running
out of something—oil, food, and strategic materials are perennial favorites. So far, however, these Malthusian outcomes remain elusive. Despite occasional scares and shortages
(remember the oil "crisis" of the early 1970s?), economic development has not yet hit the
resources wall.

But why haven't we run out of resources yet?

Malthus overlooked technology, and technology is the reason that limited natural
resources have yet to restrain economic development.

Technology operates in two main ways: The first is to increase productivity, getting
more output from each unit of input. Agriculture is a good example. The supply of land
is fixed, as Malthus knew, but technology has increased the yield per acre beyond anything
that he could have imagined. Many experts believe that agricultural productivity can
continue to rise, ultimately to a level that can support the world's growing population. Technology has similarly made the finding and exploiting of virtually all mineral and energy
resources increasingly efficient.

Second, technology contributes new products that meet our needs as well or better
than more resource-intensive old ones. For example, aluminum replaces copper in trans-
mitting electricity, plastics replace metal in our automobiles, and recycled steel replaces
virgin material in our soda cans. Telecommuting, a product of information technology,
replaces whole transportation systems in the workplace. Economic research done mainly
in the last 40 years shows conclusively that such substitutions, along with increasing productivity, account for the absence of natural resource constraints on economic development.

For technology to play this role, however, people need an incentive to use it. A system for creating these incentives contributed to preventing the Malthusian prediction—that resources will run out—from being true. The system is the free market, and its prices provide the incentive. For example, when oil supplies tightened during the oil embargoes of the 1970s, the price of all forms of energy rose. Rather than devote more of their budgets to energy, however, consumers adopted more efficient patterns of energy use. And with higher revenues, energy companies invested in new and more efficient methods of production. By the mid-1980s, energy prices returned to their long-term, downward-trending path. Most natural resources that are economic commodities—that is, that are easily traded in markets—have similar histories.

The market does not work in this way for all resources, however, because an unregulated market treats some resources as free. The capacity of air and water to absorb and dissipate pollution is the most common example. This capacity is limited, and like any other limited natural resource, technology can make it more productive. Since air and water are used without cost, however, no economic incentive exists to put technology to work. To compensate, government finds ways to limit the amount of pollution that can be emitted. In response, polluters look for ways to cut emission at the lowest possible cost. In this way, government regulation creates the incentive that brings technology to bear in managing limited environmental resources.

If sustainable development only required providing economic commodities and controlling local pollution, free markets mediated by a bit of government regulation might work for the long haul. But sustainable development faces a more difficult problem. A new, enormously influential variable has been introduced: human activities that, for the first time in the history of this planet, have changed large natural systems at an observable rate. Climate, the oceans, and critical ecosystems such as tropical rain forests and coral reefs are changing at an accelerating pace. In consequence, resource management tools that have served well up until now are not likely to keep on working at this larger physical and political scale.

One problem is that of modeling large natural systems. Crafting models useful for regulating local pollution is not too difficult, but in the case of large natural systems, it's hard to see how models can reliably predict cause and effect. The systems to be modeled may be given to discontinuities, even to chaotic behavior. The historical record seems to suggest that this is so at any rate of change, making the phenomena hard to model. Moreover, the global systems of interest are in perpetual flux, and relying on models to isolate the effect of one change from all the rest is very difficult. These systemic problems, along with the considerable time scales involved in some models, seem to me to put the verification of deterministic models pretty well out of reach.

In addition, deciding how to manage natural systems at a global level introduces a whole new degree of political complexity. Experience shows that reaching an enforceable political consensus in international forums like the United Nations is hard enough. The difficulties of managing sustainable development are more profound than even this. Involving a diversity of cultures brings to the consensus process an equally great diversity of values that people assign to benefits and costs. For example, the wealthy tend to place a great value on sustainability, while the poor are usually more interested in development. Different cultural views of the value of nature can cause other complications: Some value human dominance over nature, while others envision a more symbiotic relationship. In any case, the decision criteria seem vastly more complex than the rationalist criterion that is built into the standard policy model.

All things change; nothing perishes.

—OVID

I am not trying to argue that we should abandon the notion that benefits should be weighed against costs, or that the more productive use of resources is essential to sustainability, or that marketlike incentives can powerfully induce productivity. Indeed, I believe that these policy tools will continue to provide for the sustainable use of economic commodities and environmental resources for a long time to come. But I am suggesting that these tools may have serious limitations when applied to the class of resources that we call large natural systems.

The crucial limitation is lack of knowledge—about values, measurements, models, and consensus. As a conclusion to this book, therefore, I want to suggest some directions in which scientific research might move to provide the knowledge we need. The topics below are ones that particularly interest me as the director of an institution that studies the diversity of life and culture. Others will raise additional—and possibly more useful—questions from the perspective of their own disciplines.

In any event, and in no particular order, here are five topics in which research might well produce valuable new insights for managing large natural systems and the impacts they will feel from forces of change:

> *Establish a way to measure ecosystem health.* In 1998, at the annual meeting of the American Institute of Biological Sciences, Rita Colwell, then director of the National Science Foundation, stated: "It is not enough to explore and chronicle the enormous diversity of the world's ecosystems. We must do that—but also reach beyond, to discover the complex chemical, biological, and social interactions in our planet's systems. From these subtle but very sophisticated interactions and inter-relationships, we can tease out the principles of sustainability." And tapping into natural history museum collections for evidence of biological change will be an important part of this effort to establish an effective measure of ecosystem health.

> *Explore more efficiently for evidence of biological diversity.* The diversity of living things is declining, so time is short to create inventories of it. Since speed is important, scien-tists need to decide how to use the available time to maximize the amount of useful information they can acquire. For example, sampling strategies designed to confirm the existence (or absence) of new concentrations of biological diversity may some-times be more appropriate than comprehensive inventories of well-known habitats. Deciding how to conduct inventories is thus an important scientific problem.

> *Learn more about the functioning of large natural systems, especially the climate and the oceans.* This information might improve the performance of large models, but that is

not the best reason for pursuing it. Rather, this research can help scientists understand the characteristics of change in these systems—whether the behavior is chaotic or discontinuous, and the circumstances that govern this behavior. Because conducting experiments on these systems is often impossible, a study of the historical record of natural change seems a particularly important line of investigation for these issues. In fact such records, mostly held in museum collections, may be the chief source of data for verifying theories about the behavior of large natural systems.

Understand how to make nature and society more resilient to change. Since change is inevitable and even desirable, humanity should take care that its interventions do not create rigidities that make nature less adaptable to change. Some of my colleagues, notably Rick Potts, Director of Human Origins at the National Museum of Natural History, make a persuasive argument that human activity has a history of creating just such rigidities. As Potts suggests in his book *Humanity's Descent: The Consequences of Ecological Instability,* breeding plants and animals only to maximize agricultural productivity may risk making the food supply less resilient to a changing environment.

Explore how human cultures have incorporated values into societal behavior, especially values relating to nature. From such studies, policy makers might learn more about how to find common ground on the value of sustainable development. We might even find a way to encourage consensus to rise from the bottom up, which is almost always more effective than centrally imposed policy. Here again, a study of history should be instructive, especially the insights from cultural anthropology studies.

These are challenging questions for research, and much more. Such questions expose a critical insight—that in the sustainable development debate, science can and should shape the fundamental conceptual framework of policy. Addressing the issues that these questions bring forth requires researchers to assume a proactive role that can anticipate future problems. Science can and should lead, not follow. There can be no greater relevance of science to policy than this.

Yet another role is even more important. Whatever intellectual adventure lies ahead in meeting the new challenge of sustainable development, it seems to me crucial that scientists persistently tell the story of the natural world and of humanity's place in it. The story must be told in terms that help the public understand more fully the complexity and value of the large natural systems that sustain us. For only then can we expect the importance of sustainable development to be understood and, ultimately, implemented and practiced.

Two birds in two hands: Two conservationists—one from Madagascar, one from Europe—hold two vanga birds from Madagascar, species in need of international protection. Once the island nation was called the naturalist's promised land. Now that promise is imperiled, as it is worldwide. The course of nature is in the hands of the human species as it studies and shapes, honors and challenges Earth's forces of change.

Contributors

Edward S. Ayensu, a Ghanaian scientist and president of the Pan-African Union for Science and Technology, is former chairman of the botany department at the Smithsonian's National Museum of Natural History. He has also chaired the World Bank's inspection committee.

Anna K. Behrensmeyer is research paleobiologist and curator of vertebrate paleontology at the Smithsonian's National Museum of Natural History. She reconstructs ancient land ecosystems using geology, fossils, and an understanding of the processes of organic preservation, or taphonomy.

Daniel B. Botkin is president and founder of the Center for the Study of the Environment in Santa Barbara, California, and is a professor of biology at George Mason University in Fairfax, Virginia. He is the author of *Discordant Harmonies: A New Ecology for the Twenty-First Century* and *Strange Encounters: Adventures of a Renegade Naturalist,* as well as several other books.

Alan Cutler, a geologist and writer based in Maryland, was a research associate at the National Museum of Natural History and scientific consultant for the Forces of Change program at the Smithsonian Institution.

Gretchen C. Daily, an ecologist, is a professor of biological sciences and director of the Interdisciplinary Program on Environment and Resources at Stanford University. She has published about 150 articles, both popular and scholarly, and recently coauthored *The New Economy of Nature: The Quest to Make Conservation Profitable.* Her primary efforts focus on making conservation economically attractive.

Robert Fri is a visiting scholar at Resources for the Future, a Washington-based nonprofit dedicated to applying social science research to environmental and natural resource policy. He is the former president of Resources for the Future and the former director of the

Smithsonian's National Museum of Natural History. He also chaired a National Resources Council committee that established health standards for radioactive waste at the Yucca Mountain Repository in Nevada.

Michael Garstang is a research professor in the Department of Environmental Sciences at the University of Virginia. He specializes in tropical marine and continental meteorology of the Earth's surface and lower atmosphere.

Stephen Jay Gould was a prolific and popular science writer, best known for such books as *Ever Since Darwin: Reflections on Natural History* and *The Panda's Thumb: More Reflections on Natural History,* which won the National Book Award. Gould was the Alexander Agassiz Professor of Zoology and a professor of geology at Harvard University. For his influential writings, popularizing the concepts of evolutionary biology, Gould appeared on the cover of *Newsweek* in 1982.

George P. Horse Capture worked as special assistant for cultural resources and senior counselor to the director of the Smithsonian's National Museum of the American Indian before retiring and returning to his childhood home of Fort Belknap in 2005. The former curator of the Plains Indian Museum at the Buffalo Bill Historical Center, Horse Capture recently coedited *A Song for the Horse Nation: Horses in Native American Culture,* which features items from the NMAI collection.

Lynn Margulis is Distinguished University Professor of Geosciences at the University of Massachusetts at Amherst, specializing in microbial evolution and organelle heredity. Her most recent book, coauthored with Dorion Sagan, is *Acquiring Genomes: A Theory of the Origins of Species.* She has published many other titles, including *What Is Sex?, What Is Life?,* and *Mystery Dance: On the Evolution of Human Sexuality.* She received the Presidential Medal of Science in 1999.

William Melson is senior scientist emeritus in the division of petrology

and volcanology of the Smithsonian's National Museum of Natural History. Recently he has collaborated with archaeologists at sites in Kenya and Israel. He also studies the role of volcanoes in forming the ocean floor.

Helena Norberg-Hodge is the founding director of the International Society for Ecology and Culture and cofounder of the International Forum on Globalization. For her work in Ladakh, she received the Right Livelihood Award. She is author of *Ancient Futures: Learning from Ladakh* and *Bringing the Food Economy Home: Local Alternatives to Global Agribusiness.*

Tom O'Neill is a feature writer for NATIONAL GEOGRAPHIC magazine whose recent work has included stories on India's untouchable caste and on Celtic culture.

Jonathan Overpeck is director of the Institute for the Study of Planet Earth, a research center dedicated to fostering a new interdisciplinary paradigm among physical, biological, and social scientists. A professor of geosciences at the University of Arizona, he specializes in global change dynamics and has published numerous scholarly articles on the topic.

David Quammen, a longtime naturalist and journalist, has written a number of books and articles for the National Geographic Society. He is best known for *The Song of the Dodo* and *The Boilerplate Rhino,* a collection of essays about human perceptions of the natural world. He recently published an article in NATIONAL GEOGRAPHIC, provocatively titled "Was Darwin Wrong?" His most recent book, *The Long Follow,* documents J. Michael Fay's journey across the African continent.

Dorion Sagan is a science writer who has published prolifically both in magazines and books. He recently coauthored, with Eric D. Schneider, of *Into the Cool: Energy Flow, Thermodynamics, and Life,* and, with John Skoyles, *Up from Dragons: The Evolution of Human Intelligence.*

Illustration Credits

Eric D. Schneider is an interdisciplinary scientist whose research involves a synthesis of physics and biology. A former national laboratory director for the Environmental Protection Agency and senior scientific advisor at the National Oceanic and Atmospheric Administration., he is currently affiliated with the Hawkwood Institute in Livingston, Montana.

Barbara Boyle Torrey, visiting scholar at the Population Reference Bureau, previously served as executive director of the behavioral and social sciences division of the National Research Council, National Academy of Sciences. She has published numerous scholarly and policy papers on the issues of population growth and its effects on society.

Bernice Wuethrich, a Washington-based science writer, composed the text for the "African Voices" exhibition at the Smithsonian's National Museum of Natural History. With Henry Wechsler, she coauthored *Dying to Drink,* a book on binge drinking on college campuses. Her science and nature articles have appeared in *Science, Smithsonian Magazine,* and *International Wildlife.*

COVER
(upper left), Digital image © 1996 CORBIS, Original image courtesy of NASA/CORBIS; (upper right), Joel Sartore/NGS Image Collection; (lower left), Joanna B. Pinneo; (lower right): Grant Faint/Getty Images.

FRONT MATTER
2, Chris Johns, NGS; 5, Joel Sartore/NGS Image Collection; 6, George F. Mobley; 9, William Andrews Clark Memorial Library, University of California at Los Angeles; 12, NASA; 15, Frans Lanting; 17 (upper), Jim Brandenburg/Minden Pictures; (lower), Sarah Leen; 21, Alan and Sandy Carey.

PART ONE
22-23, Victoria Sayer/CORBIS SYGMA; 24, David Coulson/Robert Estall Photo Agency; 27 (upper), George F. Mobley; (lower), Maria Stenzel; 28-29, Joanna B. Pinneo; 31 (upper), National Geographic Photographer Jodi Cobb; (lower), from the collections of the Library of Congress, Prints and Photographs Division; 33, Gerd Ludwig; 35, David Doubilet; 37, Joanna B. Pinneo; 38, Peter Essick; 41 (both), Michael Yamashita; 43 (upper), David Leeson/Dallas Morning News; (lower), Jim Richardson; 44-45, Peter Essick; 47 (left), Nashua River Watershed Association; (right), George Steinmetz; 49, Jay Dickman; 52, Michael W. Quearry; 55, Darlyne Murawski/NGS Image Collection; 56-57, Joseph Rodriguez; 61, Robert Winslow/Earth Scenes; 63 (upper), Kenneth Garrett; (lower), Index Stock.

PART TWO
64-65, Jack Dykinga; 66, O. Louis Mazzatenta; 71, Keith R. Porter/Photo Researchers, Inc.; 72-73, Adriel Heisey; 77, Sam Abell; 81, R. Williams (ST ScI), NASA, 83, Kenneth

Garrett; 84, Dr. Jeremy Burgess/Photo Researchers, Inc.; 87, A.T. Winfree; 88-89, George Steinmetz; 93, Joel Sartore/NGS Image Collection; 94-95 (photos), National Geographic Photographer Michael Nichols; 99, Joel Sartore; 101 (left), Joe McNally; (right), Lynn Margulis; 102, François Gohier/Photo Researchers, Inc.; 105 (upper), Warren Morgan; (lower), Jonathan Blair; 109, Jonathan Blair; 110-111, Peter Essick; 113, Chris Johns, NGS; 117 (upper), Irwin Thompson/Dallas Morning News/CORBIS; (lower), Gerardo Mora/epa/CORBIS.

PART THREE
118-119, Jim Richardson; 120, Thomas J. Abercrombie; 123 (upper), Tammy Mobley LaDrew; (lower), John Page, ISEC; 124-125, 129, Thomas J. Abercrombie; 131, Robert Caputo/AURORA; 132, Edward S. Ayensu; 135 (both), Michael Kirtley and Aubine Kirtley; 137 (upper), Betty Press/Woodfin Camp & Associates; (lower), Gilles Peress/Magnum Photos; 138-139, James L. Stanfield; 143 (upper), Michael Yamashita; (lower), Luiz C. Marigo/Peter Arnold, Inc.; 144, 147, Edward S. Curtis; 151, AP Photo/Assiniboine and Gros Ventre Tribes; 152-153, Ken Blackbird; 157, Ken Blackbird; 159 (upper), Bazuki Muhammad/Reuters/CORBIS; (lower), Benjamin Lowy/CORBIS; 160, Cary Wolinsky; 163, Roger Ressmeyer; 164-165, Joel Sartore/NGS Image Collection; 169, Mark W. Moffett; 172, Maria Stenzel; 173, Maria Stenzel; 174-175, James D. Balog.

AFTERWORD
176, Mark W. Moffett; 179, Grant Faint/Getty Images; 181, José Azel; 184-185, Frans Lanting.

ACKNOWLEDGMENTS
The Forces of Change program examines the geological, environmental, and cultural processes that have shaped and continue to change our world. It consists of a permanent exhibit hall at the Smithsonian's National Museum of Natural History, traveling exhibitions, publications, interactive computer products, and public programs. The Forces of Change program has been made possible by a generous grant and on-going support from the National Aeronautics and Space Administration.

The W. K. Kellogg Foundation, the U.S. Department of Agriculture, the Mobil Foundation, Inc., the American Farmland Trust, the Environmental Protection Agency, and the U.S. Global Change Research Program have also made important contributions to the Forces of Change project and to this publication. Forces of Change received invaluable support from many people. The NMNH project team would like to thank the following people in particular for their help, their hard work and their encouragement: Pamela Baker-Masson, Bruce Falk, Robert Fri, Bob Harriss, Felix Lowe, Carolyn Margolis, Robert Sullivan, Herman Viola, Judy Mannes, Marsha Rehns, Becky Tarbotton, Bee Wuethrich, Don Edwards, John M. Eger, Terry Evans, Robert W. Kates, Annette Olson, the Olson family, Tom Veblen, Nick and Luz Cutler, Terilee Edwards-Hewitt, Tom Lindsey, Barbara Tilghman, Sarah Skorupski, Beth Rosenberg, and Anne Hall.

Index

Boldface indicates illustrations.

Public health: Africa 137, 140
Punctuated equilibrium 70
Purple bacteria 96
Pythagoras 85

Q

Quaternary extinction 104; see also Late
    Quaternary extinction
Quaternary Extinctions (Martin) 108
Quinine 36, 37

R

Rabgyas, Tashi 129
Recycling: Ladakh region 126; metals
    181
Red River, Minnesota 148
Reid, Walter 173
Relating to nature 19, 20
Religious beliefs 18
Reproductive system changes 162, 163
Reptiles: extinction 166
Rich, Adrienne 96
Rio de Janeiro, Brazil: watershed 172
Rivers 46, 48
Rosy periwinkle 36
Round River, Wisconsin 46, 48

S

Sahara Desert, Africa: giraffe carvings 24;
    Sahara Dust Layer 142–143, 143
Salmon 6
Salt crystals 12
San Jacinto River, Texas: floods 43
Sand dunes: High Plains 30, 31
Saskatchewan River, Canada 148
Scales of change see Timescales
Schopf, William 60
Schrödinger, Erwin 92
Schrödinger's paradox 92
Seafloor spreading 54, 58
Second Law of thermodynamics 86–87,
    90, 97
Serengeti grasslands, Tanzania 130
Sierra Nevada mountains, Colorado:
    megadroughts 32
Siuan family 147
Slavery 136
Snakeweed 37
Solar energy 53, 91, 92
Solina Beach, California 22
Solvent, water as 40–41
South America: continental drift 55;
    El Niño 33; marsupials in 54
South Big Horn Creek, Montana 156
Species: ecosystem services 167–168;
    extinctions 166, 167; number of 166
Spirochetes 100
Sri Lanka 158
Steadman, David W. 112
Steam engines 87, 90
Steinbeck, John 25, 106
Stoddart 47
Storms 116–117; water cycle 42
Sturgeon River Gorge, Michigan 38

Sulfide 96
Sulfur cycle 162
Sumatra, Indonesia 158
Sumbawa Island, Indonesia: Tambora
    Volcano 59
Sunyata 122, 126
Surface winds: El Niño 33
Surgical advances 134
Sustainable development 177–178,
    180–183

T

Tambora Volcano, Sumbawa Island,
    Indonesia 59
Taphonomy 82–83
Tuareg people 29
Tawney, R. H. 108
Technology: in Africa 133, 134, 140–141;
    and balance of nature 11; changes in
    Ladakh region 122; evolution of
    humans and 98; functions of 178;
    incentives to use 178, 180; iron smelt-
    ing 134
Teilhard de Chardin, Pierre 60
Theater, idols of 68
Thermodynamics 85–98; adaptation
    exploiting energy sources 91; closed
    vs. open systems 86–87; defined 86;
    First Law 86; gradient-reducing traits
    90–91; in living organisms 90–91;
    metabolism 97–98; original applica-
    tions 87, 90; Schrödinger Paradox
    92–93; Second Law 86–87, 90, 97
Thoreau, Henry David 20
Timbering 110–111
Timescales 67–80; catastrophism 74–78;
    classic error of scaling 69; deep fallacy
    of 78–79; evolution 69–71, 74–75;
    human time 68, 70–71, 75–80; magni-
    tude of difference between 69–70;
    and moral questions 76–77; and para-
    dox of visibly irrelevant 77–78; and
    permanent apocalypse 78; planetary
    time 68, 70, 71, 74–79; punctuated
    equilibrium 70; uniformitarian view
    71, 74–76
Tornados 90
Triassic extinction 104
Tribe, idols of (Bacon) 68, 69, 71
Tsunamis 158, 159
Twain, Mark 67

U

Uniformitarian view 71, 74–76
United States economy 34
United States South Seas Exploring
    Expedition (1838) 13, 14, 20
Unsustainability 178
Urbanization 50–51

V

Value of nature 181
Vancouver, Canada 179
Vanga birds 184–185

Venus: atmosphere 93
Vernadsky, Vladimir 93, 96
Vesuvius, Mount, Italy 80
Vidae Falls, Oregon 174–175
Vietnam: sustainable harvests 171
Virunga National Park, Democratic
    Republic of the Congo 94–95
Visibly irrelevant, paradox of 69–70,
    77–78
Volcanoes 58–59; effect on climate 59;
    gases from 52, 59; interior 9; between
    North and South America 54–55

W

Wallace, Alfred Russel 107
Water 39–48; erosion 42, 46; evapora-
    tion 41–42; floods 39–40; as force of
    renewal 42, 46; fresh 40; molecular
    properties 51; rivers 46, 48; as socie-
    tal/environmental issue 40; as univer-
    sal solvent 40–41
Water cycle 42
Water vapor 42
Watershed protection 172, 173
Weathering 42, 46
Whale watching: California 5
What Is Life? (Schrödinger) 92
Whitman, Walt 14
Wicken, Jeffrey 91
Wilkes, Charles 13, 20
Wilkes Expedition 13, 14, 20
Williams, George 70
Wilson, E. O. 166
Wilson, Harold 136
Winds 142
Woolly mammoth 105

Y

Yellowstone National Park, U.S. 21;
    Grand Prismatic Spring 88–89

Z

Zebra mussel 58
Zimbabwe: ecotourism 171
Zortman Mining Inc. 154

Forces of Change

Published by the National Geographic Society

John M. Fahey, Jr., President and Chief Executive Officer

Gilbert M. Grosvenor, Chairman of the Board

Nina D. Hoffman, Executive Vice President;
  President, Books Publishing Group

Prepared by the Book Division

Kevin Mulroy, Senior Vice President and Publisher

Leah Bendavid-Val, Director of Photography Publishing
  and Illustrations

Marianne R. Koszorus, Director of Design

Barbara Brownell Grogan, Executive Editor

Elizabeth Newhouse, Director of Travel Publishing

Carl Mehler, Director of Maps

Staff for this edition

Susan Tyler Hitchcock, Project and Text Editor

Meredith Wilcox, Illustrations Editor

Claudia Costas, Illustrations Specialist

Diane Nelson, Art Director

Michael Horenstein, Production Project Manager

Staff for previous edition

Kevin Mulroy, Project Editor

Patrice Silverstein, Alan Cutler, Text Editors

Sadie Quarrier, Martha Davidson, Illustrations Editor

Bill Marr, Art Director

Rebecca Hinds, Managing Editor

Gary Colbert, Production Director

National Museum of Natural History

Barbara Stauffer, Project Manager

William Melson, Don Wilson, Melinda Zeder, Science Advisors

Manufacturing and Quality Management

Christopher A. Liedel, Chief Financial Officer

Phillip L. Schlosser, Vice President

John T. Dunn, Technical Director

Vincent P. Ryan, Director

Chris Brown, Director

Maryclare Tracy, Manager

Founded in 1888, the National Geographic Society is one of the largest nonprofit scientific and educational organizations in the world. It reaches more than 285 million people worldwide each month through its official journal, NATIONAL GEOGRAPHIC, and its four other magazines; the National Geographic Channel; television documentaries; radio programs; films; books; videos and DVDs; maps; and interactive media. National Geographic has funded more than 8,000 scientific research projects and supports an education program combating geographic illiteracy.

For more information, please call
1-800-NGS LINE (647-5463)
or write to the following address:

National Geographic Society
1145 17th Street N.W.
Washington, D.C. 20036-4688 U.S.A.

Visit us online at
www.nationalgeographic.com

For information about special discounts
for bulk purchases, please contact
National Geographic Books Special Sales:
ngspecsales@ngs.org

The Library of Congress has cataloged the earlier edition of this book as follows:

Forces of change : a new view of nature / Daniel Botkin ... [et al.].
    p. cm.
    Includes bibliographical references (p.)
    ISBN 0-7922-7596-9
        1. Natural history. 2. Earth. 3. Human Ecology. 4. Global environmental change. I. Botkin, Daniel B.
QH45.2 .F67 2000   99-087996
508–dc21   CIP

Copyright © 2006 Smithsonian Institution
All rights reserved.
Reproduction of the whole or any part of the contents without permission is prohibited.

ISBN-10: 1-4262-0017-X (regular edition);
          1-4262-0018-8 (deluxe edition)

ISBN-13: 978-1-4262-0017-5 (regular edition);
          978-1-4262-0018-2 (deluxe edition)